THE DIAMOND PROCESS™
Using Everyday Triggers to Awaken the Treasure Within
Veronica Krestow

The DIAMOND Process

© 2015 by Veronica Krestow

All rights reserved. First edition 2015.

Disclaimer and Rights

ALL RIGHTS RESERVED. No portion of this book may be reproduced by any mechanical, photographic, or electronic process, or in the form of a phonographic recording; nor may it be stored in a retrieval system, transmitted, or otherwise be copied for public or private use—other than for "fair use" as brief quotations embodied in articles and reviews—without prior written permission of publisher.

The purpose of this book is to provide helpful information and inspiration. While all the stories and anecdotes described in this book are based on true experiences, all names of clients have been withheld to protect each individual's privacy.

While the author and publisher have used their best efforts in preparing this book, they make no representations or warranties with respect to the accuracy or completeness of the contents of this book and specifically disclaim any implied warranties of merchantability and fitness for a particular purpose. No warranty may be created or extended by sales representatives or written sales materials.

TABLE OF CONTENTS:

Dedication	4
Is This Book For You?	5
Getting The Most From This Book	6
Chapter 1: My Story	8-17
Chapter 2: The Power Of The Present Moment	18-21

PART ONE: INNER PURPOSE

Chapter 3: Discovering the Diamond Self	22-29
Chapter 4: Beyond the Mind and Ego	30-39
Chapter 5: What is Inner Purpose?	40-49
Chapter 6: What is SHINE Time?	50-61

PART TWO: A SEVEN-WEEK TRANSFORMATIONAL JOURNEY

Chapter 7: Awakening the Diamond Self - *Week 1*	62-79
Chapter 8: Setting an Intention - *Week 2*	80-99
Chapter 9: Awareness: Seeing Triggers as Treasures - *Week 3*	100-119
Chapter 10: Using Medicinal Dialogue - *Week 4*	120-143
Chapter 11: Making an Offering of Forgiveness to the Past - *Week 5*	145-161
Chapter 12: Relaxing into Nothingness - *Week 6*	162-175
Chapter 13: Declaring Your Destiny - *Week 7*	176-191

PART THREE: THE DIAMOND PROCESS

Chapter 14: The Seven-Step Transformational Process in Action	192-213
Chapter 15: Lead Your Life With Love	214-233
Acknowledgements	234-235

This book is dedicated to the unshakable,
unbreakable Love that lives within you.

PREFACE

Is This Book For You?

Dear Precious Friend,
Deep down inside yourself have you ever felt like you have a greater reason for being alive? Do you sense you have something magnificent within you that wants to bloom? Are you too busy, anxious, or just tired of trying to keep up with life to find your way into discovering and expressing your magnificence?

Do you practice yoga, meditate, or even splurge on regular massages, yet deep inside yourself you still feel stressed, sad, or irritated? Are you in the middle of a frightening transition and need guidance as you struggle to find your way through it?

Have you been attracting the same disappointing drama no matter what you try to do to get away from it, which has been distracting you from genuinely standing tall with confidence?

What if there was a better way available for you *Now*? What if this better way allowed you to feel strong, centered, and rooted in life as the authentic you regardless of what is going on around you? Would you say "yes" to it?

Whether your answer is "yes" to all of these questions or you can relate to just one of them, this here book has been designed to serve as a space of sanctuary for you. Within these pages you'll find the help that you need to discover who you truly are, come into further alignment with your unique destiny, and lead your life with love.

Welcome to your transformational journey.

INTRODUCTION
How to Get the Most From This Book

Some of my deepest moments of wisdom have come from spontaneously pulling a book off of my bookshelf and flipping to a page. The journey of truth and awakening is not linear. It is wavy, marvelous, and unpredictable. Above all else, follow your inner-guidance whether that means reading this book cover to cover in one sitting, flipping to a page and pondering a few sentences for days, or loyally completing one step per week as a 7-week course (as offered in Part II). Just like life, you can't get it wrong. Yet, in order to get the most out of this book, I do invite you to read the whole book and implement the exercises provided.

Together, we will be moving through the Diamond Process, a 7-step transformational experience that's been designed to support and free you during moments of pain, confusion, or great challenge. As you practice this process it will serve as a catalyst of your awakening into true power. What we are given in any circumstance can either serve us or enslave us. I am deeply inspired to share this transformational journey with you, supporting the liberation of your true self... the Diamond Self.

In Parts I and II of this book, you will discover and experientially practice the 7 steps of DIAMOND as stand alone gems. Then, in Part III of this book, you will be given the full Diamond Process technology so you can implement this process in your own life. This is where you will have the opportunity to break through a current challenge in your life and step into Freedom. In the final section, you will have the opportunity to discover how you can lead your life with love, joyfully make a beneficial difference in our world, and join the Diamond Community to support you along your inspiring, authentic path.

Repeatedly woven into this transformational book, you will notice a practice called SHINE Time which I created for you as a nourishing opportunity to pause and activate the Diamond Self... your true self. I will explain this more fully in Chapter 4. For now, please know that this simple practice of SHINE Time in and of itself has the power to bring you to a state of Inner Peace, Clarity, and True Confidence immediately.

Challenges are gifts...
and triggers are treasures.

Challenges are gifts... and triggers are treasures.

"It is by going down into the abyss that we recover the treasures of life."
Joseph Campbell

Why I Am Writing This Book

When I was two years old, I witnessed something a little girl should never see. My beautiful, intelligent mother fell apart, rapidly descending into mental illness. I also watched as, against her will, she was forcibly taken away in a straight-jacket (that's how they rolled back then). At best it was a dramatic event that was terrifying and confusing for a small child to witness.

She was unique, my mother. A beauty queen in Miami Beach, she wasn't just pretty, she was also running for congress in our town. She was a captivating woman with soft, turquoise eyes, a thick, blonde mane, and a strong, hourglass frame. I can't tell you how often I witnessed the jaws of both men and women actually drop in response to her stunning beauty. Everything about her, from the way that she dressed, to the way she talked, to the way she moved, easily conveyed to all that she was an expert at poise and maintaining a perfect image.

However as the years went on, I became terrified of my mother. In living with her, I was privy to what boiled beneath her enviable surface. It seems to me that her madness had simply grown tired of hiding behind her beauty, designer clothes, and that smile that could - and often did - light up a room.

Her episodes ranged from crawling around for hours on end, convinced she was a cockroach as she made strange clicking sounds with her lips, to buying $2,000 (which was an obscene amount of money back in the 80's) worth of karate clothes only to hang them all around the house like Christmas ornaments. Every night, my loyal father came home to a very different woman. Who would she be tonight? Would she be a regressed two-year old who threw dishes around the kitchen laughing and free? Would she be seething in anger waiting to blow up on him as he walked through the door? Would she be gardening and peaceful, standing as the loving wife and mother he fell in love with before they married? I'm sure that he always hoped for that last possibility that would finally pull him out of this horrendous nightmare, but it never did.

Over the years I grew to see my mother as a disaster... someone that I swore that I would never become. Yet during this same time I found myself putting my loving, stable, predictable father on a pedestal. As the nightmare ensued, and my mother's insanity continued to grow, my father's patience eventually collapsed and their marriage transitioned into a radical split. I was only five years old at the time, yet I was still forced to make a very grown up decision; do I live with mommy or daddy? However much I loved my mother, the choice between an earthquake or a refuge was easy for me to make. I chose the refuge.

At any given hour of the day I could tell you exactly where my father was... he was dependable to the "t." Conversely my mother was a wild, tameless force who often terrified and infuriated me as she would appear, unexpectedly and unannounced, and more often than not, embarrass me with her strange ways. It didn't matter where I was... at school, a friend's house, or even my karate class. She would show up out of the woodwork and I never knew what she was going to be like whenever she did. She was the shadow that I could not run fast enough to lose, while my father was the lighthouse I always hoped would illumine me.

At a very early age I learned to view the emotional, wild feminine, as demonstrated by my mother, as a sickness. For this reason I spent the first 20+ years of my life unknowingly shaving away these genuine parts of my authentic self, simply because they remotely resembled this person who was my mother. Eventually, I got so good at running away from what I didn't want to look at that I managed to escape across the country to California, where a promising life awaited me.

Even though I got away from my mother almost entirely, my own insanity silently grew within. Even after a graduate degree in psychology and mentoring with cutting-edge leaders in the field, it wasn't until I managed to create the perfect body, a passionate partnership, the five-star lifestyle and even a burgeoning career that I began to hear, feel, taste and touch a wild pain within me that my polished life could no longer hide. It was as if the prettier my life got, the uglier and more worthless I felt inside. The more divided I was. The bottom line was I became an expert at running away from myself. In desperation, I finally realized that my only real solution to finding true peace and claiming a great life was to run towards myself, and embrace everything that I'd splintered off... wildness and all.

However, instead I kept running. Like most people, I was running away from myself in the guise of creating a great life. Yet, deep down something felt off and I felt lost, unseen, misunderstood, and powerless. I was often anxious, feeling like a victim of circumstance, as I measured my value by the approval I worked so hard to receive from those around me.

No matter how great my success, deep down inside myself I continued to hear,
"I can't."
"I am unable."
"I'm not good enough."

Something was constantly nagging within me that created an inescapable itch under my own skin. Nothing made sense. I was on the verge of marriage and deeply in love. I looked the best that I'd ever looked, and had all kinds of degrees and experience. I'd even studied with leading pioneers in the fields of psychology, spirituality, metaphysics, and yoga. As a result, I had a path paved before me that looked promising indeed. Yet, the reality of my situation was that no matter how hard I tried to get away from it, there was nothing I could do to avoid the dark side, the shadow of my own self. I found myself in a constant state of battle, not only with my partner, but

in my life overall. I was afraid... afraid to make decisions because I was afraid that they'd be the wrong decisions. I was afraid of getting married. Afraid to give full commitment to my work. Afraid to face my community and ask for the support I needed. Afraid to show up powerfully. Afraid of falling apart. I knew that I couldn't say "yes" to a life that was so bountiful and beautiful until I faced the lack and ugliness within me. I knew that I needed to find my truth and so this is where my story of transformation really begins.

BEFRIENDING THE WHOLE OF ME

As you may know from following my Youtube channel, in 2009, after spending some time deeply searching my soul, I walked away from a glorious life that I'd spent years carefully building. I went on my own journey into the redwoods, where I finally had enough silence to hear and befriend the pain, the anger, the confusion, and yes - sigh - even the depression! Even now it feels so good to openly use the word "depression" in relation to myself. For my entire life, I saw that word as a negative label, a branding... a disease. I felt that if I ever even remotely identified with this label, that it would be with me forever as a hell that I would never escape.

Today, I know differently. Today, I know depression as a friend - my friend - and a wise one within. It's a facet of myself that says, "Hey! This is not okay! Speak up for yourself. Choose what you want. Turn within. Stop giving in!" As I discovered on my journey in the redwoods, depression, like anger, grief, or any of the other "negative" emotions we face, are all friends. Yes, they are friends of the soul and as such are facets of life's guidance system that say:

"You need to go left. Now! Stop... you're moving too fast."

"Excuse me? You were just betrayed. Someone just stepped over your boundaries and that's not okay."

"I'm hurting. I need love. Please hear me."

These are all communications from deep, deep down within and as I went on this journey in the redwoods, I finally faced each facet of myself, one by one, as the emotion spontaneously arose. As I said, I was too ashamed to communicate transparently with my family, friends, and loved ones. Most of the time I didn't feel understood and every response that I received, even when I shared from the depths of my vulnerability, left me feeling weaker.

On those rare occasions in which I'd begin pouring out my heart, I'd invariably be interrupted with:

"Why don't you do (such and such) to get happy?"
"Why don't you try (this or that) in your relationship to make it better!"

These well-intended responses felt like someone was scrubbing salt into my wounds. However good the intentions were behind their remarks, I felt more lonely and irritated than ever. It was then that I began to realize how hungry I was to be heard and to be held... silently... compassionately. Each opinion varied so far from the next one that I felt torn apart even wider - and into even more pieces - and my jagged confusion continued to grow.

As human beings, when we are confused, we are divided... insane. Insanity has become the status quo in our culture. I am not talking about diagnosed pathological dysfunction. I am talking about that light, crazy hum that's pulsing through today's society as the norm. As modern people, we have lost an ancient truth and as a result we have forgotten who we really are. We're caught in our own minds and drowning in judgment... of ourselves, our families, our friends, our culture, our past, our futures, our waist lines, our leaders. What's right? What's wrong? Who's pretty? Who's not? Who's wearing the right clothes? Who isn't?

The list goes on and on. Yet what if there was a better way?

AWAKENING TO THE PRESENT MOMENT

During this time when I was alone in the redwoods, I was able to get so very still. I was surrounded by so much love with the trees, the clean, silent air, and the roaring ocean. In this stillness, incessant judgment and thinking began falling away and no matter how challenging at times – alright, MUCH of the time- I was simply left with whatever I was genuinely feeling and experiencing. Moment to moment. The freedom was astounding.

The weather patterns kept changing. First rain and hail, then sun and wind. In Mendocino, California, the weather is in a state of constant change. What I discovered there is that I was seeing a reflection of my own wild feminine; my own boundless expression that is never stagnant for long. All of my life I had been judging my wildness from a place of fear. For some reason, I felt that if I were to be me, this woman with feelings and a lot to express... with all colors of the spectrum that included a boldness, a softness, and everything in between... that I would either be put away, thrown away, or locked up, just like my mother.

As you can see, going to the redwoods and finding my soul's truth was an extraordinary part of my journey. It was also during this time that I discovered the **Diamond Process**.

HOW THE DIAMOND PROCESS WAS BORN

During my time in solitude I found myself constantly moving through a series of steps out of sheer necessity. I kept doing this again and again... *and again*... to feel and heal (which really proved to be synonymous) all of the emotional energy that was rising to the surface within me.

In this spacious, loving, private atmosphere it was easy for me to feel everything, no matter how hard, ugly, or toxic the feeling. I felt an immense sense of relief in finally being able to express myself instead of keeping everything deeply buried as I'd been doing for decades. It felt so freeing to hear myself, in varying tones and vibrations that I didn't even know were in me, now that I was finally free of other people's perspectives and entanglements.

In traveling through what has since become the **Diamond Process**, I began to recognize a pattern of clear steps that I was repeatedly taking to set myself free. They were my refuge and provided a reliable structure while everything within me was falling apart. Every day, something new would come up - if not multiple things - to sit with, be present with, and give a voice to. Every day, I went through the same process to let go and break through. As I tracked this distinct pattern, the **Diamond Process** was born, becoming an amazing resource and my most trusted ally.

Eventually, like the polishing of a rough diamond, I refined my process so powerfully that by the end of nine months I was able to move through a feeling, challenge, limitation, or block with so much Care and Presence. In fact there were times when it was effortless. Like breathing, it simply became a part of me, a lifestyle that mid-wifed my soul and freed me into the Present Moment, nurturing the whole, loving woman that I came here to be.

As I strengthened my ability to sit with all facets of myself that I had previously avoided, I grew grounded, rooted, and present in situations that had once made me tremble. Other people had less of a hold on me. I could show up as myself... vulnerable and quiet, or loud and boisterous. I learned to welcome my complexity, the whole of me. In other words, I got my life back.

Today, life is no longer scary or burdensome as it once was. Life is a gift. Everything is a gift when we know how to unwrap it. When you consciously move through the inner-domain of darkness and pain, everyday life challenges, whether big or small, become manageable and maybe even exciting.

Maybe. The irony is that in facing the darkness in me that reminded me of my mother, I became the unshakable stability I had so admired in my father. Now, don't get me wrong, by no means did I become perfect. I simply stopped trying to be perfect. This is when I realized the perfection inherent in my imperfections.

When we awaken the Diamond Self within our hearts, anything is possible within our lives. Rather than running away by trying to perfect ourselves, we slide into home base, purposefully and playfully choosing to be here in this moment, becoming the source of love we have been waiting for. Imagine having a genuine, unwavering acceptance of yourself and others that no one can give you and no one can take away. How would your life be different?

SHARING THE TREASURE

Once I'd finally reclaimed my life, I eventually started working with clients again. As I began working with others, I discovered that this process was not only applicable to me, but I was also able to share it with clients and witness a consistent, liberating transformation in them as well. You can imagine the excitement I felt in seeing that the value extended way beyond my own healing. My own healing would have been enough, so this was a generous surprise.

Helping people migrate from debilitating anxiety to living inspiring, interdependent lives, which is very common in my work today, became a natural extension of my own transformation. Through the years, I have had the great privilege of witnessing people in dark depression eventually arise from it renewed, excited about life, clear, resourceful, and fully able to move forward. I've seen great expressions of anger dissolve into tears, laughter, and love. I've witnessed careful, quiet women courageously free their voices and dreams. I have seen so much raw, indescribable beauty take shape in myself and others, and at the same time, whatever I have yet to see, I trust that Presence has the power to hold, honor, and heal.

As for my love life, I honestly never imagined opening my heart to another in committed relationship. I was afraid to fail again, even though I hadn't failed to begin with. I also felt so much love and security within myself that I didn't have the same need to merge with someone. Yet, life clearly had another plan. I fell in love with a man I was friends with for years. I moved back to Los Angeles to be with him while simultaneously **taking the leap into sharing the *Diamond Process* globally through small, intimate webinars.**

To say that the ***Diamond Process*** changed my life is an **understatement.** It saved my life. I am certainly not saying this book will save **your life or that** you can't live without it.

However, what I am saying is that within it, there is great **potency that can** put power back into your heart, true genius into your **mind, and** limitless creativity into your hands so that you can naturally lead your life, with LOVE, through anything.

"Brilliant. Resilient. Authentic.
Clear. Infinite...
The Diamond Self lives at the
core of every human being."

> *"Praise and blame, gain and loss, pleasure and sorrow come and go like the wind. To be happy, rest like a giant tree in the midst of them all."*
>
> Gautama Buddha

The Power of The Present Moment

At 31, I was living the "good life" in Los Angeles. I was madly in love, radiating perfect health, establishing myself as a successful integrative healer, traveling around the world first class, living in a multi-million dollar home, and surrounded by people who loved me. On the outside, my life looked like a living fairy tale, yet deep down I felt lost. My life on the surface, however shiny and substantial it appeared to be, felt empty.

So, as I previously mentioned in chapter 1 of this book, I left. I left everything I knew behind, including my cherished boyfriend of 6 years, our home, my city, community, material belongings... everything (except, of course, my sweet kitty, Stella)!

For over a year, I lived alone in the quiet of the redwoods, grieving the life I was leaving behind and the persona I had spent a lifetime building in search of answers to burning questions like,

"Who Am I?"
"What is the purpose of my life?"
"Why do I feel so bad when my life is so good?"

This time of solitude, however confronting, was a great privilege, an experience that completely transformed my life and opened my eyes to the True

Purpose of life and a clear, simple path to living it, which is why I am writing this book for you.

Today, I understand that I was given the gift of having everything life could offer early on (yet still feeling unsettled inside) so that I could realize that what we, as human beings, most need can only be found within our hearts once we **wake up** to the Present Moment. Putting the Present Moment first is the key to stepping into our True Power, discovering who we really are, and actualizing our full potential.

People often ask me *"What is Presence, Veronica?"* They also often ask me, *"How do I know if I am in the Present Moment?"* Living in the Present Moment is actually very simple, which is why it is so easy to overlook within such a complex world. If you can hear, see, taste, touch, or feel it, then it is here and part of the Present Moment. In other words, your five senses are not only how you determine whether you are in the Present Moment or not, but they're also a direct way of returning to it.

Anything other than what is tangible in the Now is a thought, which at the deepest level, contrary to popular belief - gulp! - doesn't even exist. If you are thinking about the past or someone you were interacting with yesterday, you are in your mind and outside of the Present Moment. If you are dreaming up a great future or are worrying about a situation that may happen tomorrow, next week, or a decade from now, you are also in your mind. Living in the mind nearly all of the time, which is where most people dwell this day in age, leaves one feeling lost, drained, and alone. Although, it is necessary to plan for the future and occasionally think about the past, it is essential to befriend the Present Moment and hang out here regularly if you want to thrive.

To put it simply, when you are thinking and hypnotized by the incessant voice in your mind, you have left the Present Moment, your true Home, which is what has created so much anxiety in our humanity. Thanks to my teacher, Leonard Jacobson, and his enlightenment teachings, once I started to grasp this simple, yet essential truth, and make the Present Moment my priority I began to meet who I truly am for the first time and, holy goddess, has life become magnificent!

This book is designed to invite and guide you into the Present Moment, too, so that you can avoid the heartbreak I went through in striving for and then arriving at the ideal life only to realize I had missed the point completely. My deepest prayer for you is that by adventuring into this book, you will tap into the great power of the Present Moment, where everything you truly seek can and already is coming to life. The fact that you have attracted this material says that you are ready to wake up and further deepen into the power of who you truly are. I celebrate you and all you have already

experienced on your unique path that has led you to arriving here.
Welcome Home to the miraculous world of the Present Moment.
I am grateful you are here.

THE DIAMOND PROCESS

I created the *Diamond Process* to help you return Home to the Present Moment, your only - yes, only - point of true power. This is the place where your deepest need is always fulfilled. Since living in the Present Moment is essential to being clear, centered, radiant, confident, and peaceful, it is imperative to find a way of being established in the stability of the moment rather than painfully lost in chaotic thinking and fear.

Yet if having a still mind and living in the Present Moment were easy, we would all be living Buddhas, Ghandis, and Christs, embodying our true potential as souls, right? As our world is showing us, the reality is that there are countless obstacles to overcome and without a constructive way of moving through them, life can feel like an exhausting ride to nowhere. The good news is that the challenges can actually be fun to navigate. More importantly, from our soul's perspective our challenges are actually gifts in disguise.

I have created the *Diamond Process* as a simple, practical system to help you ease into the Present Moment, shine through suffering, and fall in love with your authentic life. Recently, in my final session with a client whom I'd worked with privately in conjunction with the Love-inar Journey, she looked at me with a huge smile. As the tears welled up in her eyes she quietly said these beautiful words to me, *"I am excited to live."* After a couple of months of witnessing her feeling so defeated by life, suddenly seeing the brightness in her eyes and the sincerity of her joy only affirmed the power of the Present Moment that's revealed in the 7 Steps that I'm sharing with you here in this book.

The *Diamond Process* is a tested formula that celebrates one of Nature's Laws: challenges promote growth, evolution, and resilience. As human beings, we can either collapse beneath obstacles or rise up, seeing them as disguised opportunities to awaken. The *Diamond Process* invites you to consciously embrace the **Whole** of who you are, with no exceptions, and empower yourself to shine even brighter for the Highest Good of All.

Although challenges are simply part of the path, struggling does not have to be. I am sharing the *Diamond Process* with you to help you relax into the Present Moment and awaken the empowered, authentic, radiant being you are here to BE with ease and grace.

You are a diamond.
You were born valuable.
This journey is designed to dust off
anything in the way of you
remembering... who you truly are
and shining as unbreakable Love.

PART ONE
INNER PURPOSE

Chapter 3 - Discovering the Diamond Self

Chapter 4 - Beyond the Mind and Ego

Chapter 5 - What is Inner Purpose?

Chapter 6 - What is SHINE Time?

> *"Your task is not to seek for love, but merely **to seek and find all the barriers within yourself that you have built against** it."*
> Rumi

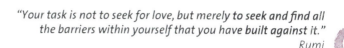

Discovering The Diamond Self

When Michelangelo was asked about the process of creating his breathtaking masterpiece, "The David," without hesitation he gave his answer. He simply explained to his questioner that the angel was already inside the marble and that his only duty was to chisel away the excess to set him free. At our core, we too, are masterpieces, waiting to be set free from the excesses that hide our true beauty.

Yet the reality is that we can be so distracted by the incessant fluctuations of our lives. Countless ever-changing thoughts circle around in our heads like the debris inside a tornado. This random "thought debris," like daisies, dust, home appliances, rooftops, and cars spinning inside a storm, doesn't make much sense, but still, it surely commands our attention. It's because of all this "debris" that we singularly and blindly focus on the never-ending up and down daily drama that we call "life," which causes us to lose sight of who we really are... the still, peaceful center within.

What was it about Michelangelo that allowed him to see such magnificence within the full potential of what that boring block of rock was asking to become? Most people would walk by that very piece of raw marble, seeing nothing but worthless stone. It takes **Presence**, **Heart**, and **Vision** to see beyond what meets the eye... to sense and feel a little bit deeper.

Michelangelo's angel lives in each of us - a precious, masterful beauty at the very center of our beings. This is what I call the **Diamond Self**; a radiant, still **Presence** that is infinite in nature. But, how do we set it free and how would your life change if you fully accepted that there is nothing to add to yourself to become something exceptional? How would your life shift if you discovered that you already are clear, strong, brilliant, loving, and peaceful within your core?

Most of us spend our lives striving to become something great while completely forgetting that, at the deepest level, we already are what we seek. In our innocent ignorance we bury our greatest value beneath a set of false beliefs and disempowering expectations. We are all miracles designed to actualize, only the carving tools are not in someone else's hands and the miracle does not involve waiting for someone else to swing the hammer against the chisel. For each of us, the chisel is one of love and the true miracle is your perspective... your consciousness... the **Diamond Self**, available in the heart of **Now**.

THIS MOMENT IS YOUR THRONE

During my time of solitude in the redwoods, I disconnected my cell phone, had no schedule, and allowed myself to fully experience myself, and life, moment by moment. I was living on two acres of land filled with trees, a natural pond, deer, bunnies, birds, skunks, bob cats, raccoons, banana slugs, lizards, salamanders, mountain lions, you name it. Wildlife was all around me. It was my own personal Walden Pond.

In the center of the woods there was one old-growth redwood that had been cut down some thirty years prior, leaving a large, flat stump. Over the years it had been cushioned with layers of old leaves and silky mosses. In a nearly perfect half-circle around it stood eight young trees, forming the perfect throne that had been naturally "designed" for the queen of the forest. It was here where I created a small mandala out of stones, sticks, feathers, greenery, and added fresh flowers daily. After weeks of sitting on the ground in front of it for my morning meditations, I suddenly realized that this "seat" was for me. It had never before occurred to me that I could actually sit on this grand, natural throne.

I will always remember that morning. In the

heart of silence, I stood up from my meditation and effortlessly glided toward it as if something else was beckoning me in the same way that something mysterious breathes me without any doing on my part. There was no thought, just an impulse to rise, walk, sit, and lean back into this welcoming majestic throne.

In the arms of the "Communitree," this community of eight trees, I learned to let go, be held, be loved, and be mothered into a queen. Day after day, I'd return to this Communitree like a little girl... straight out of bed with tasseled hair and make-up free. For the first time in my life I allowed myself to be raw, honest, and trusting enough to totally drop the pretty mask that I'd worn for so many years. Some mornings I cried in gratitude for this privilege, while other mornings my mind was spinning with anxiety and fears about the future. There were even occasions when I raged and wept and even spontaneously sang hymns like a tameless force as I forgave my past and everyone in it, especially myself.

Even in the face of all of my moods, all of my facets, the Communitree remained exactly the same. Calm. Compassionate. Accepting. Loving. Present. The **Presence** in these woods was undeniable. No matter how strange this all seemed to my mind, in the deepest sense of the word, I had found **Home**. This was the mother that I had unknowingly prayed for all of my life. Now I finally understood anew the term of endearment, "Mother Nature."

There was nothing to prove anymore, not even to myself. There was nothing to control, no person or circumstance to fight against, and no thought from which to escape. Nobody knew where I was. I had no one to answer to, and no obligations, expectations, or "shoulds." In this peaceful setting I experienced a radical falling away of the layers that had held me captive, lost in my story, and apart from my True Nature, and the honest Present Moment.

It was during those months with the trees that my **Diamond Self**, the true me at the center of my being, began to awaken. I started to see what was right in front of me with 100% attention and feeling, rather than being occupied by anxious thought. I could sit with a leaf or a dewdrop resting on a blade of grass for hours on end, the way that I'd done as a very small girl. An entire world, one that I'd been blind to for three decades, re-opened in my very **Presence**.

I felt like a camera that'd had its lens cap on, thus never seeing anything. I could see that I'd been like this for nearly my entire life. Arriving in the woods allowed me to finally remove the cap from my lens. The longer I sat in these woods, the wider the aperture opened letting in more and more light. Every time I shifted my focus from thinking to simply *being* with what was right in front of me, I relaxed. I had found my way into the sweet secret of life and this relief brought me to my knees, which is where I began to discover even more miracles.

I was amazed at how much life there was in a few square inches of dirt. I found ants, worms, rocks, and these sparkling bits that seemed to be like natural confetti. In this same space a decomposed leaf was returning itself to the soil. I couldn't help but touch it all, and as my hands grew dirty, my heart simultaneously cleansed herself within the sea of wild exploration. I discovered how life was recycling itself in the endless cycle of life and death that actually fueled its endless expansion. As I sat with nature my whole understanding of right and wrong began to dissolve.

One morning I was present with an adorable, bright green inch worm when out of nowhere a spider landed on it, killed it, and carried it away... just like that. I felt such pity for the inch worm. Then hours later I was showering only to realize there was a spider at my feet spiraling into the drain. The predator had become prey. This is simply the glorious dance between life and death, which up until this point, I had been fighting to no end.

I laughed in the shower as I let go of this idea that I actually knew what was best. A bigger picture began to open up as if I had been pasted to the ground my whole life and now I was lifted to the peak of a mountain where I could see from greater altitude.

This greater altitude is the perspective of the *Diamond Self*, a way of seeing the world that is beyond right and wrong, beyond opposites, a state of being that reveals the oneness of everything and is 100% focused on, loyal to, and trusting of, the Present Moment.

YOUR INNER ESSENCE IS RADIANT, AUTHENTIC, AND FREE

Children are quite sophisticated. Without even knowing it they naturally embody the *Diamond Self*. As an example, have you ever noticed that when a child or animal enters a public place, the majority of people become drawn to watching or interacting with them? Their spontaneity, presence, and innocence inspires and commands intrigue. Children show us what it looks like to be free, fully engaged, and awake to what is right in front of them and that freshness stirs something deep within our souls.

Although we are no longer in brand-new, little bodies, the qualities of trust, originality, celebration, and magic, are still seeded within us. The innocent inner-child, or what I refer to as the *Inner Essence*, is a direct doorway to accessing, activating, and remembering the *Diamond Self*, the original, boundless, incomparable beauty that is you. Through the journey of this book and beyond, I invite you to become curious about your *Inner Essence*, the child within, whose senses are fully awake and creative life force is flowing bountifully.

You may be reading these words, thinking "the child within"? I am not asking you to believe anything I say, only to explore through the course of this journey what helps you more fully return to the "authentic you."

Even if it seems like reality and the world out there somehow broke your magic wand and child-like nature years ago, the truth is, the **Diamond Self** is unbreakable, still whole and intact. Even the word "diamond" itself means unbreakable. Through living in a world of noise and conflict though, it was only natural to lose touch with your still, present, vulnerable essence. By the way, when I say 'vulnerable', I do not mean weak. There is a vast difference between weak and vulnerable.

THE POWER OF VULNERABILITY

Being vulnerable is actually a form of true power. It takes vulnerability to show up in an unpredictable world of unconsciousness and suffering, allowing yourself to be fully exposed, real, bruised, and beautiful, and at the same time open enough to totally receive life and risk everything.

In a world where nearly everyone is blind to what is unfolding before them, in spite of being locked in their thinking, the flowers still bloom. Life goes on. Miracles continue. The question is, do you choose to see, even if it means being the only one genuine and present, or do you keep fumbling in the dark in order to belong?

Just as "The David" was revealed by removing the excess, part of this journey involves removing your own excess. You'll do this by going back in time to reach your hand through history, and pull the brilliant, loving child that's buried within out of your own rubble and into the light of today. In reclaiming your primary essence, you will not only discover your innate gifts and unique design, but you'll also heal and let go of the blocks that once kept you feeling lost and stuck. It sounds sweet and good, exciting and holy, doesn't it?

Yet, I can hear you now... *"How do I go about doing this?"*

Keep on reading and I'll show you how.

This moment is everything.
It is the answer to every prayer.
It is the Beloved in form... sweet...
simple... ordinary... and in such
simplicity... it is also extraordinary.

> *"Out beyond ideas of right-doing and
> wrong-doing, there is a field;
> I will meet you there."*
> Rumi

Beyond The Mind and Ego

Every time I offer a workshop, retreat, private session, or Love-inar, I always begin by clarifying to the client or group that this space is for them, the **Whole** of them, which is beyond right and wrong! I lovingly welcome every facet of who they are to be seen and held and their radical truth to be heard, which includes their deepest pain, fear, and suffering. Almost immediately, the energy relaxes and any pretense or habits of guardedness drop. Honesty begins to pulse herself open into the space of love that we co-create together. The expansive shift is palpable.

The norm in modern culture pushes the opposite. It models strength as the ability to be in control, holding it together, and being immune to fear and pain, even if the cost is hiding behind an imprisoning facade. Even though it is our true nature to let go and be free, the pressure of fitting in tends to override the impulse to be authentic. In looking at my own masks and methods of pretending in the world for over a decade, I have become very intimate with the mind and ego. As a result I've gained pure insight into why we humans generally tend to bury parts of ourselves, making it impossible to feel seen and at home in the world, even with our closest loved ones.

Since awareness is power, in this chapter we are going to explore what typically stands in the way of embodying the **Diamond Self**. In looking at what has blocked your full expression and potential, you can then make space for what frees you into it.

Let's start from the beginning, the very beginning ...

IMAGINE...

You are a precious baby only a few days old and fully engaged in what you currently see, hear, taste, touch, and smell. Life is fascinating... and foreign. You have just come out of the warm, dark womb where you were fully held and connected to the source of life through your mother. Now, you are breathing your own breath within an indescribably vast space, and looking out through your own eyes at a bright, new world.

You are present and you were born this way... a baby Buddha or Christ. You are awake, conscious, pure, entirely free of thought or identity, and totally in awe. Your mind is open and silent.

Silence... your native origin... the Home that today you may not even realize you are longing to be once again. Yet within a world of so much chatter, noise, drama, and opinion, where does such spaciousness fit in?

As small children, even when the world around us was noisy, our minds were silent, rational thinking hadn't developed yet. Rather than interpreting language, we felt the energy behind it. We didn't think about it. We didn't plan. We just experienced what was right in front of us as it was happening, moment by moment.

Somewhere along the way, of course, the mind and the ego develops and we learn to leave Home, the **Present Moment**, and begin thinking our way into the world of concepts, comparisons, and time. Rather than being predominantly awake to the **Present Moment**, and only occasionally exploring the world of thought, we unconsciously jumped head first into a sea of dreams, beliefs, and memories, completely abandoning and forgetting the land of Now and who we truly are.

So many of us feel lost, disconnected, and abandoned by life, loved ones, the Universe, and by God. What if this is simply a projection, mirroring the way we left the **Truth** of life by over-thinking our stories and abandoning what is real - what is right in front of us? What if this could be solved by simply reconnecting with **Life** again, including **Nature**, our loved ones, and all that is tangibly here and now, especially ourselves and our own hearts? What if finding our way **Home** was as simple as making the ever-available, totally-loyal **Present Moment** our priority again? What if feeling into it, like a sacred lover you would give anything for, is all we really needed to do to be free again? To the ego, this is a ridiculous thought, or it may not even make sense... yet. To the ego, the only salvation lives in bettering your story, making more money, finding the right relationship, getting in better shape, landing the amazing job, which are all versions of improving yourself and your life. That is all good and fun to play with so long as you know this alone will never lead to lasting peace. What I am inviting you to is This Moment and who you are right now. Is this enough? Are these words enough? Is your heart beating enough? Is the scent in the air enough? Is this breath enough? Is where you are right now in this precise moment worthy of your attention? Is what you can feel, see, taste, touch, and hear right now enough for you? Are *you* enough... now?

There is no right answer to these questions, by the way, other than your honest response. In looking at and genuinely answering these questions, and exploring your relationship to the **Present Moment**, whether they make you feel frustrated or exalted, a freeing insight is starting to stir within you.

EMOTIONS AND THE PAST

One of the main blocks to being **Present** and thriving, are repressed emotions from the past. Within our society, we have been so conditioned to repress negative emotion, to medicate depression and anxiety for example, which is simply a symptom of a deeper cause. In running away from negative emotions like fear, anger, depression, shame and guilt, we simultaneously run away from ourselves, our inner guidance, and you guessed it - the **Present Moment**... our only point of power.

Often, people ask me if emotions are considered part of the **Present Moment**. Even though, you can't see, smell, or taste an emotion, you can certainly feel it in your body. Any emotion you can feel in this moment is part of the **Present Moment** and just as worthy of attention as the flower sitting on your desk or a baby crying to be fed.

Often times, repressed emotion from the past will rise up into the **Present** to be released. Growing up in a world where we are typically encouraged to hold back the tears, or hide our anger and upset, these emotional energies inevitably get stored in the body. What would naturally take two minutes to express, we, instead, fearfully hide and unknowingly hold onto in our tissues, muscles, and organs for twenty, thirty, forty years and beyond. The journey of awakening into the **Present Moment** involves releasing these energetic packets of pain as they naturally resurface so that we can free ourselves and lead our lives with love.

Under the ego's rule, painful feelings are buried. Keeping painful emotions locked down is actually one of the key methods the ego uses to ensure you are more accepted by those around you. The only problem is that in repressing feelings from the past, we get lost there, harboring old emotional baggage in the physical and energetic bodies.

It's like shamefully lugging around trash sacks filled with heavy rubble that's been collected through the years, weighing us down from walking lightly, confidently, and freely. It requires a lot of energy to fight down these feelings that are designed to be set free. The habit of burying feelings keeps most of us locked within the repressed, reactionary toddler's world, protecting unhealed wounds, terrified to feel much at all, blaming others, feeling unloved, and quietly (or sometimes not so quietly) resenting life in the process.

The beauty is that if we shift from reacting to circumstances to actually looking at ourselves, and sifting through this baggage that we've been dragging around, becoming radically honest about what we feel and need as we do, we activate an inner spark that can blast us off into a new and inspiring reality. The moment we say *"yes"* to loving ourselves and putting our own self-care and radical self-acceptance first, is when we step off the "hamster wheel of disempowerment" and head for the sunset.

However, most people are so accustomed to clenching their jaws and fighting against life, even while they are desperately praying for peace, that they can't see the path that can easily take them there. The ego tries to control life, as it thinks that it knows best. The **Diamond Self** drops the fight completely, opening up to an unknown greater possibility.

Our day-to-day environment, as well as the company we keep, play a huge factor in whether we shut down or open up in the face of life's inevitable triggers, which are in fact, the doorways to our freedom in disguise. Regardless of how much money you have; regardless of the state of your health; regardless of whether or not you have a loving, encouraging support system, these pages are designed to be a form of good company that can help you soften and see the path in the midst of your life's current circumstances. You are the one you have been waiting for and rather than getting sucked into the drama all around, you can pivot your focus, look within your own heart, and lovingly take dominion over your life and wellbeing.

All war, greed, and imbalance in our world stems from a stubborn unwillingness to take personal responsibility for our own pain and suffering, things that every human carries around like the heavy bags of rubble I referred to above. Yet the good news is that once you are aware of this tendency in yourself, you can be free from it and be a living example of peace, which is who and what you are at your core.

Let's explore back in time again ... how did we lose touch with this peaceful core?

Now let's jump ahead to the age of two. You're totally relaxed and lying in the grass holding a caterpillar in your open palm. You're awed by it's tiny, seemingly-infinite legs that tickle your skin as it slowly, but steadily crawls from your wrist to your thumb. In that moment, you are entirely present with what is right there in the palm of your hand. You are awake, a living Buddha or Christ, free of thought and filled with curiosity when suddenly - BAM! Your mom storms out of the house screaming your name, in a punishing tone. In an instant, you fall from peace to paralyzing fear, your true state robbed as the hand that feeds you simultaneously snaps you out of trusting the moment. Yet more importantly, it also snaps you out of trusting life as well.

While such an event may seem insignificant to an adult, to a child who has yet to develop cognitively and is solely based in emotions, this experience can be traumatizing.

Maybe your teeth chatter or tears begin to shed. These are natural biological responses that honor and shake off the moving fear. Left to it's own devices, the subtle trauma and fear will flow through and be gone in two minutes flat. But, instead, as fate would have it, your mother's tone escalates at the site of your tears,

"We are late again!"
"Look at you. You're a mess. Stop crying!"
"We have to go now... NOW!"

Just like that, a belief is formed. Crying goes in the bad pile and rather than being expressed and set free, it gets crumpled up, packed away, and that's how the ego begins to reign supreme, building its role as your protector from pain. Those once-healthy emotions are diverted, sentenced to a life of repression where they are forced to hide, fester. and crystallize into r.u.b.b.l.e... or those "repressed unconscious beliefs and blocks of locked emotion."

As a result of these early painful experiences we spend our lives trying to construct a castle on a land mine of "rubble," only to discover that even within palace walls a feeling of fear and angst pervades.

Reading these words as a functioning adult, this may seem far-fetched to you, but I assure you that it was something to the two-year old who's a wide open receiver that's devoid of censorship, while learning at light speed about "right" and "wrong."

This goes into the good pile, that goes into the bad.

THE TROUBLE WITH AVOIDING THE R.U.B.B.L.E

The ego looks at heavy emotions as a nuisance, or something to avoid. Similarly to the powerful sun, the **Diamond Self** is still, radiant, and awake. No matter what is presenting itself, it's always shining and accepting in the *Here* and *Now*. As the sun doesn't discriminate between weeds and flowers, the **Diamond Self** is present with all emotions and sides of our personalities, serving as an ever-present refuge of acceptance and loving compassion.

As we can see, the ego, on the other hand, lives in the world of thinking, assessing, and chopping life into ideas of right and wrong. The ego, a bit like the rubble encasing "The David", serves to protect the **Diamond**, but also keeps it shrouded, and thus incapable of shining into the world. Contrary to popular spiritual belief, the ego is not the enemy. It was simply born to craft and support your identity, or the character you play in the world of time, while also serving as a mechanism of protection and defense.

When brought to consciousness, the ego's role can actually be transformed into something higher... an ally that supports liberation, well-being, and peace in your life. We'll get to this soon enough.

Even though the ego is programmed to select the "good" and reject the "bad", until we recognize and accept every facet of ourselves and learn to honor and allow our emotions, we will continue to be haunted by sides of our humanness that we'll reject. While the battles and triggers we attract from all around us bring up pain, in reality they're designed to help us notice the old hurts we have been guarding and battling within ourselves so we can heal.

Have you ever wondered what happened to all of the emotions that you've been conditioned to repress? If they weren't cried out, shaken off, or yelled up years ago, where did they go? What happens to our hearts when we learn that joy is good, but grief is unlovable, that being nice is welcome, but being fierce or angry is not okay?

The reality is, feelings are feelings. They move through us like rivers leading to one ocean. We all know what happens to our ecology as we dam the rivers. Fish die off, habitats fall off balance, and species become extinct. In the same way, when we dam up our emotions, we risk getting stuck and slowly, but surely barricading our own pathway **Home**. So, how do we return to flow, and in doing so return to our true, natural, thriving habits again?

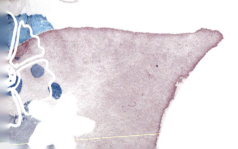

ANGER AND DEPRESSION

Each emotion carries it's own texture, tone, and purpose. For example, anger is like a rapid river that's flowing strongly and deliberately towards the vast ocean of **Freedom**. Anger is not bad in itself, but it is outrageous. It moves quickly and wildly. Anger surges in the face of violations, both big and small, from those around us as well as those we impose on ourselves by not honoring our own boundaries. Even though anger isn't designed to harm us, when stacked with judgment and shame, the anger frustratingly recedes inward adding to the hell we find ourselves in.

Depressed people have typically talked themselves out of anger and their deepest needs one too many times, damming their emotional river and thus stifling their life force. I have seen client after client *feeling* guilty for the genuine anger that is within them, skirting around expressing it, especially the highly spiritual ones.

Nice people don't want to hate or resent others. Yet, naughty or nice, we have all had very real feelings of anger at one time or another. A great metaphor for anger is fire. In fact, in and of itself fire is not a bad thing. When you are sitting around a fire, it keeps you warm and cooks your food. On the other hand, when left unattended, fire can be devastating. Similarly, when you leave your anger unattended, it can become explosive and harmful.

Just this morning, I watched a client get outrageous and speak the unspeakable as she finally freed her long-buried anger. She was initially resistant as she attempted to divert what she was feeling by giving me dizzying details about the previous night's drama. As soon as I had her pause and breathe into what she was feeling in her body, I watched her tightened jaw clench harder before bursting into a roar so large and freeing it immediately led her to tears which minutes later led to hilarious laughter. Rather than clenching onto her anger by thinking endlessly about the events that triggered her, she dropped it altogether, fully feeling what was truly rising up without being defined by it. These moments of liberating the *Diamond Self* are golden moments indeed.

My teacher, Leonard Jacobson, says if we come into right relationship as a humanity with our own anger, war would cease to exist. Yet, out of fear and ignorance, we continue to dump it or bury it, blaming others or shaming ourselves. Anger paired with blame spells **DISASTER**. Anger paired with shame spells **DEPRESSION**! When kept unconscious, when buried out of shame, anger lurks, gaining strength behind the scenes. What was once an innocent upset builds into a furious monster, waiting for just the right (or not so right) moment to free itself.

Maybe you overhear someone gossiping about you in your office. Anger's natural response is sheer destruction because it wants to kill. When someone rolls their eyes at you, anger reaches for the sword. Again, anger is outrageous. It is not logical or practical. Anger is vertical. It gets us up on our feet to stand fiercely. Yet without a healthy expression of anger, one falls flat on their face.

So, what is a healthy expression of anger and what can we pair anger with, so that it spells **FREEDOM**?

Alchemists will tell you that it only takes a speck of gold to transform a brick of lead into gold itself. One, little speck. Anger is like lead. If it can exist with a bit of acceptance in the mix, a new quality is created. It's called freedom.

Rather than unconsciously reacting to life violently by fighting and increasing the negativity on our planet, each of us has the power to make peace within. We do this by consciously choosing to see and accept all parts of ourselves, while responsibly allowing the energies of anger, pain, joy, fear, and everything in between... the full spectrum of our feelings... the freedom and dignity to complete their expression through us like rivers headed towards the sea. This isn't something we solely do once. This is a lifestyle that sets us free, again and again, restoring wellness, balance, and **Presence**.

THE MIND AND THE FUTURE

One of the key ways the mind and ego represses difficult emotions is by dreaming about a pain-free future. We become hypnotized by the promise of something better tomorrow that pulls us completely out of our only point of power, the here and now. Since *the moment* is all we actually have, that day never comes. So like everyone else, we spin on the wheel year after year, avoiding the Now, and sweating our way to nowhere by chasing mirages and dodging ghosts that we can never outrun.

If you are to wake up and claim your diamond destiny, you have the opportunity to face what has stood in the way of your freedom with courage, acceptance, and love. It will take something higher than our own egos and personal agendas to resurrect such a possibility. Compassion, Awareness and Radical Self-Acceptance are golden. It will require at least one speck of gold to shine bright at the heart of the r.u.b.b.l.e. The good news is that everything you need is already within you. You have the power to let the challenges wake you rather than break you by migrating to your unbreakable **Diamond Self**. In the chapters that follow, I will show you the difference while inviting you to experientially discover such strength, freedom, and purpose for yourself.

The building you are in right now, your lover, your friends, your bank account, your job, even your body, everything in your life is eventually going to disappear. This may seem like bad news, but when you actually embrace this, a sigh of relief so freeing will escape you as the infinite miracle that stands the test of time enters your life and never disappears. The savior, the true miracle worker, the angel, even the ultimate Love lives within you right now. Just as "The David" was always within that hunk of marble, so is the **Diamond Self** ready for liberation. Finding your way **Home** to the beloved **Diamond Self** is what I refer to as **Inner Purpose**.

> "When you lose touch with **inner stillness, you lose touch with yourself. When you lose touch with yourself, you lose yourself in the world.** Your innermost sense of **self, of who you are, is** inseparable from stillness. **This is the I Am that is deeper than name and form."**
> Eckhart Tolle

What Is Inner Purpose?

Have you ever noticed that even if you have a great **Outer Purpose** in life, like being a mom, running a company that you love, or creating inspiring works of art, that you still find yourself in an exhausting cycle of stress, anxiety, and worry? Given the modern go-go-go culture, this is the norm today. However the good news is that your reading of this book is evidence that you are ready for a much more empowering approach to life.

The reality is that in order to thrive with your Outer Purpose, your Inner Purpose of being Present in the moment needs to be tended to above all else. Without prioritizing Inner Purpose, you can still become successful with your goals, whether they be creating a lucrative business, having a fit body, or whatever else your Outer Purpose drives you to do. Yet in spite of this outward success, depletion, anxiety, and stress will remain your inevitable companions in the process. This is the ever-present experience of the majority within our world today.

WHEN GOD(DESS) COULD CARE LESS

A couple of years ago, I was in the South of France attending Leonard Jacobson's *Presence* Retreat. The beauty of this retreat was that much of it was devoted to deepening in both Silence and the Present Moment. As part of an exercise at one point during the retreat, we were asked to form small groups. In my group I began sharing some deep, raw truths about my life that were particularly centered around my business. Suddenly, within this circle of about twelve participants, Leonard interrupted me by interjecting,

"Veronica, God could care less what you do with your life, so long as you are Present!"

Gulp!

It took a moment for me to fully digest his words. When I did a huge laugh burst forth from my heart, followed by tears that streamed uncontrollably down my face.

RELIEF!

Such a sense of relief overcame me. Was I really not expected to ***do*** something great and impressive with my life? After a long, emotional pause I realized that I could live in a tree, work cleaning toilets, let my body go, or even be alone and penniless, because ***none of it mattered.*** No matter what I ***do***, I would still be me... a worthy and lovable human being. What matters most is the state of my mind and how authentic and present I Am moment to moment. This may sound simple... because it is! Isn't truth always simple? For me, though, it finally sunk in - down to my core. With this realization, the depth of relief that I experienced in that moment was completely mind-blowing and fully heart-opening!

Having a dream for the future, coupled with a belief that it will be better once you achieve it, is one of the great tricks of the ego. The ego is designed to keep one locked in a state of avoiding a painful past and running towards a better future. The authentic Self, or what I call the ***Diamond Self*** knows that the ***Present Moment*** holds the key to what you truly want and is the one and only doorway into living the relaxed, prosperous life you are here to live!

I once worked with a cutting edge healer and international speaker who came to me because deep down inside she realized that even though she was gifted in her field, and people saw her as brilliant and powerful, she never felt like she was enough. For this reason she over-delivered in her work by constantly giving even though she was barely getting by. This core belief that she was not enough kept her in a cycle of inner depletion and financial debt. While she was initially terrified to share this out loud with me, finally realizing that I could see beyond the story that was keeping her stuck allowed her to feel safe with me.

As we dug deeper, we finally identified the origin of this pattern within her that she wished to heal and release. At 9 years old, her family, who had been reasonably wealthy, uprooted themselves from South America and moved to the States. As with many immigrants, they were starting over again. As a result they had relatively little money, yet they still insisted that their little girl attend a private school, which just happened to be posh and privileged. In this new situation, not only was she poor in comparison to her classmates who sported designer clothing, but she was also a "foreigner" with a heavy accent and a unique way about her.

As a result, the popular girls at school made fun of her and over the course of two years, she transformed from a joyful, confident child to someone who was self-conscious and ashamed. While she eventually found her way out of that school and into a group of friends she felt safe with in a public school, the belief that she was not good enough was still imprinted within her subconscious. It was the power of this belief that kept her anxious and cautious beneath her smiles, even within safe circumstances.

This is a perfect example demonstrating how the ego naively steps in to create a happy life without first tending to the source of pain. Like throwing a party dress over third degree burns, it doesn't work. For my client, no matter how good her life got, even thirty years later, underneath all the trappings and accolades she continued to be haunted by a part of herself that needed love and tenderness.

Over time, she learned to soften her mind and embrace the wounded child within, putting the **Present Moment** and her own **Wholeness** first, above that of her clients and everyone else. This gift to herself also became the foundation of being able to be of healthy service to others, something many healers today could benefit from.

Over the course of several months, she started valuing herself more, giving and receiving in balance, which also helped her get her finances in order. In learning to prioritize her **Inner Purpose** she was able to stay recharged rather than draining her life force by worrying, over-doing, and over-thinking. Instead of being lost, running toward a future that would never be enough, she became loyal to the **Moment**, where she found herself to be more than enough, as she is **Now**.

When you prioritize the **Present Moment** as your Inner Purpose, anything un-

resolved in your heart will come up to be embraced and accepted. The good news is that these unresolved pieces are no longer viewed as a burden, as these perceived nuisances actually become avenues for deepening in **Presence** and blossoming. When you can be the one you have been waiting for, carefully unfurling the party dress and patiently tending to those burns, big and small, life begins to deliver the very gifts you have been calling in.

What happens to your body, your heart, your mindset when you declare the following? This moment is enough. I Am enough right now. I Am waking up to the liberating world of Now.

I trust the still sanctuary within me.

STILLNESS, SILENCE, AND INNER PURPOSE

There is a source of Stillness within you which all ideas, forms, and manifestations spring from, including Outer Purpose which we will get to in Part IV of this book. It is within this nourishing space of Inner-Silence and Stillness that we regenerate and recharge, which leads to relaxed, inspired action, yielding the most prosperous outcome in our lives.

Have you ever noticed that most people are taking action out of stress, worry and anxiety, perpetuating a draining cycle? Maybe you even see this in your own life? In a world of incessant movement and noise, it is up to us to find our own rhythm by pausing regularly, not just when you put your head to the pillow at night, but periodically throughout the day in order to touch and plug into the ever-abundant, peaceful Source within. From there, practical solutions to every day challenges arise on their own accord, in addition to soul insight and viable next steps.

I have noticed in my own life how seamlessly everything works out when I override my old habit of taking action out of fear or restlessness and, instead, ***pause*** in the Stillness, resting in my ever-glowing Diamond Self. Sometimes it takes two minutes, other times it requires two hours free of technology, reclining quietly under a tree, allowing my story to fall away for a while. The insights that arise from the simple, silent pauses always lead to the highest outcome, without fail. So long as I have the courage to let go completely first (which is where embodying Self-Mastery comes in and what the **Diamond Process** empowers), I inevitably bloom. Flowers, butterflies, rivers... everything in nature requires a letting go to flow and evolve into such majesty. We are the same.

THE DIAMOND SELF

Like a glorious lotus planted within a meditation pond, inside the word "diamond" lives the letters **I-A-M**. This is what yogis and sages have referred to as the IAM *Presence* for centuries. Mooji, a great living Guru says, *"The intuition "I AM" is your truest name. Love, joy, peace and wisdom are your real nature. This is true for all living beings. But, you will not fully know and be this until you are willing, open and ready to go beyond your personal identity into Truth."*

The I AM is the essence of Inner Purpose, a state of Being that we all are at our cores, a still, silent, awake state of mind beyond personality, name and form. Attuning to this deeper Truth within leads to a radical sense of purpose, oneness, and peace. It is our Home. It is the Source we were born out of and the source we will dissolve into when we leave this life. Yet, we don't have to wait until physical death to embrace it. Awakening to the Present Moment is how we begin to touch this inconceivable, boundless dimension.

The Silent *Presence*. The infinite, eternal source of life that witnesses all that is, moment by moment, through your individual lens is the IAM *Presence*. This *Presence* is available Now. It doesn't celebrate or oppose. It just is. It doesn't try to prove anything to anyone. It just is. It doesn't try to save the world. It just is. It doesn't attempt to improve or become better. It already is. Even as the personality of you moves in the world and perhaps even strives to be the best you can be, the I AM remains unchanged, devoted to the business of Is-ness.

In the land of ego, however, the IAM *Presence* is worthless until it has a list of accomplishments following it that fill in the "blank" to proving it's purpose and earn it's right to be alive.

I am a good wife.
I am a stellar businesswoman.
I am the world's greatest father.
I am going to change the world.
I am rich.
I am poor.
I am respectable.
I am a disgrace.
I am getting there.
I am falling behind.

The list goes on and on, depending on mood and quality of mind in any given moment, which as we know changes like the weather. However foreign to the ego, Truth lives in the still space prior to filling in the blank and beyond the labels that categorize you and everyday life. **I AM.** Before going

on to read the following paragraphs, how does it feel to simply pause and breathe into these two words as they are?
I (inhale) **AM** (exhale).
I AM.

How was that for you? Did you skip over the pause? Did you breathe deeply into it? Is all of this familiar and comforting to you? Is it annoying or seemingly pointless? Fortunately, there is no right or wrong answer, just your *authentic* response, which is the doorway into freedom.

THE PLAY OF CONSCIOUSNESS

One simple way to open up to the world of the *Diamond Self* is to see it as a passive witness. This witness simply watches life unfold as an innocent audience member **(IAM)** enjoying a show, while the personality that is you plays your role within it, believing it is real. The Yogi's call this the "Leela," the play of consciousness. We are here to dream, to play, and eventually to wake up to our True Self in the midst of it all. Thus in the face of doing and believing, we're choosing to return *Home* to *Being*.

Rather than being the one on stage who is spinning through tragedy and comedy, the I AM, the core of the *Diamond Self* is merely watching the play, free of thought, criticism, or judgment; with a full surrender to the reality that the play is simply happening. It is like watching clouds passing through an open sky with a full understanding that the clear blue sky is the only constant, untouched by the temporary, passing patterns and fluctuations.

What happens when you have believed your entire life that you are the clouds, only to realize that you are the infinite sky behind what you thought was you?

When you can witness the unfolding of life with the same sense of surrender, neutrality, and *presence* that you feel while watching the clouds spontaneously roll by, you are living your *Inner Purpose*. If you can touch this deeper dimension of you even for as little as a couple of minutes a day, the ego begins to lose it's grip as your consciousness is set free like a river rushing *Home* to the great *Sea*.

You know you are touching this miracle when the mind is quiet, it is as simple as that. In those moments of such profound Inner-Silence, you are wide awake, riding the waves of life rather than being crushed by them in your exhausting attempt to control them. Rather than thinking about life - be it other people's opinions of you or your opinions about them - you become free and focused on what truly matters.

TRUE POWER IS ALWAYS AVAILABLE TO YOU

In every single moment we have the power to be awake. Even if you have been lost in thinking, gossiping, or worrying for the last three weeks, or even the past thirty years of your life, the most important thing to realize is that **ONLY THIS MOMENT MATTERS.**

ONLY. THIS. MOMENT. MATTERS.

This moment holds the key and has the power to consecrate every year that has come before this one. As soon as you let go of past and future, fully embracing the truth of Now - whether the sound of wind rustling through leaves, the phone ringing, or the itch on your shoulder - you are fulfilling your *Inner Purpose* to shine within your own *Being*... to be *Home* in the *Stillness* of *Now*.

Touching this state of *Being* within, which is always available to you, awakens the ultimate freedom and a deep cellular trust that all is well. As you shift from thinking about your life to whole-heartedly enjoying and witnessing life, free of thought, free of words - silent, present, and aware - the infinite joy of being on purpose awakens. This is *Inner Purpose* and it becomes both easier and more natural over time.

This is a radical returning to Truth... a falling away of the rubble... a diving deep into the diamond heart of *this*. Just this. It is primary and comes before anything else, including Outer Purpose and living your destiny path. Had I known this prior to working to create such a beautiful life back in Los Angeles, I never would have needed to give it all up. I wouldn't have even needed to leave to the redwoods. I AM the redwoods. From this place of connection to *Inner Purpose*, the redwoods, the unshakable sanctuary is always within. I AM *Home* herself and so are you.

Being in touch with the I AM *Presence* within is the ultimate purpose, as everything that is meaningful and fruitful naturally arises from this awakened, spacious way of seeing the world. From this perspective, you can see the leaves on the tree, yet you are not thinking about the age of the tree or what species it is. You simply see the color and shape. You feel the breeze on your face. You watch the squirrel zipping by. The sunshine and you become *One*. You are *One*. The aliveness of everything becomes palpable as your worries cease to exist.

From the **I AM** *Presence*, there is zero agenda - not even to thrive - but simply to witness and genuinely respond when necessary, allowing the mystery of *Life* to unfold *Herself* with absolute grace and messiness perfectly combined. The **I AM** is where ***Oneness*** can be felt and remembered, where we all radiate from the ***Source***, shining bright at the heart of **DIAMOND**. It is where the yogic greeting *"namaste"* originates. The light in me recognizes the light in you. The silent spark of consciousness within me bows to the silent spark of consciousness within you.

Touching this sacred dimension is pure liberation, a remembering into our own divinity. It's Michelangelo's angel standing firm and still as all of the rubble around him shatters and falls to dust. It's like dropping into a deep, warm sea, slowly feathering all the way down past the surface waves, through the chill, to the still, ocean floor. It is ***Home***. It is ***Boundless***. It is ***Love***.

The ***Diamond Self*** is a magical, essential state. It cannot be seen or measured. It is the seer. Grounded. Silent. At the center. Of everything. And nothing. Just like dropping into ***Presence*** while moving through our day to day lives, once we land at the base of the ocean floor, so to speak, we can still see the activity of fish and flowing sea plants around us, boats motoring above us, and sunshine refracting through. Yet from this vantage point we are centered in ***Silence*** and ***Stillness*** where peace prevails. It is here where life loses it's hold on you. There is an overwhelming sense of being cared for as well as a sparkling gratitude for being alive.

Inhabiting this dimension of being is so simple that we almost always miss it, getting lost behind the surface noise of our day to day doingness. Our primary purpose for being here, our ***Inner Purpose***, is to remember... to see... to feel... to hear... to taste... and to touch life. This moment is ***everything***. It is the answer to every prayer. It is the ***Beloved*** in form... sweet... simple... ordinary... and in such simplicity, it is also **extraordinary**.

Just this.

Being Present is the greatest gift we can give our souls, each other, and especially the Beloved Creator. It is our Inner Purpose. As scientists say, we are made of stardust. Everything is. As the mystics say, the stars gave us eyes so we can see our infinite nature twinkling and reflecting back in the evening sky.

We are infinite.
We are consciousness itself.
We are living, breathing miracles.

The good news is that you don't have to prove or earn your right to wake up to this miracle. You don't even need to understand any of these words. The beneficial energy behind what I am sharing with you is what has actually attracted you to exploring this material. Some part of you is ready to remember your Inner Purpose and, in truth, you are receiving exactly what you need from this very book just by having it in your hands.

The **Present Moment** and your **Inner Purpose** is always available and ever-present behind the noise, to do's, and story lines of your life. It is the way **Home** - a return to Love - and you are holding the key within you **Here** and **Now**.

Ready to open the door?

> *"The secret of change is to focus all of your energy, not on fighting the old, but on building the new."*
> Socrates

What is SHINE Time?

If you are yearning to discover your **True Self** and actualize your **Inner Purpose**, yet you don't know how, I have wonderful news for you. During my time in the redwoods, as I began awakening to the exquisite dimension of the **Diamond Self**, I found an immediate, simple way of blossoming into the **Present Moment**.

The following transformational practice is one that I discovered while sitting in solitude in the heart of silence amidst the trees. This practice, something that I call SHINE Time, is a delightful, accessible way to awaken the **Diamond Self** that reveals more and more benefits to you as it's practiced over time. SHINE Time is a simple, reliable practice that returns you **Home** to the still, radiant sanctuary within you. You can use it any time and any place. When practiced regularly this practice has the power to transform your life. Ideally you are best served to begin doing this every couple of hours for a few minutes at a time. Yet, eventually it becomes effortless as you rest more and more into the **Present Moment** and who you really are.

SHINE TIME

SHINE is an acronym:
STILLNESS
HEALS AND
ILLUMINATES
NATURAL
ENERGY

STILLNESS HEALS AND ILLUMINATES NATURAL ENERGY

Let us begin with *"S"*: *Stillness*. As mentioned in the previous chapter, *Inner Stillness* is how we connect to *Inner Purpose*, the key to leading a flourishing, empowered life. This isn't about stopping or resisting thoughts, although coming into physical *stillness* is certainly beneficial. This is moreso about witnessing the movement of thoughts from a *Still*, *Centered*, *Awake* place. It is about activating the witness... the **I AM** *Presence* that we explored earlier.

The easiest way to come into *Stillness* is to pause your body and mind from doing and engaging with the outer world (i.e. stepping away from technology, other people, etc.) while focusing your awareness on your breath. As you read these words, for example, I invite you to inhale deeply... and then exhale slowly. Now, you are migrating from outer activity and thoughts about others, what you need to do later, or even this book, to the tangible sensation of your breath entering and exiting your body.

As if you are reeling your lines back into the boat at the end of a fishing trip, bring in all lines of thought, all lines of energy, and all lines of doing back into your body... like rays returning to the sun on the wings of your breath. As you inhale, receive your energy back into your self, bringing your awareness, quite simply, to your body. As you exhale, feel your body relax into *Stillness*.

STILLNESS HEALS AND ILLUMINATES NATURAL ENERGY

Now, for the letter *"H"*: Healing. The word *"healing"* is derived from the word **Wholeness**. When we come into **Stillness**, we return to **Wholeness**... our **Home** where nothing is lacking and all is well. I like to think of coming into **Stillness** as a way of plugging into the ultimate **Source** of energy and power in the same way we plug our cell phones into an electrical socket. When we come into **Stillness**, we are healing, refilling our cups so that we may move forward from the overflow.

Much of the time it only takes a few minutes of genuine **Stillness** to recharge completely. Just a few minutes ago as I was writing the previous sentences, I suddenly got very heavy and tired. My mind wanted to fight it by saying, "It's only 1:50 p.m. I shouldn't be tired. Something must be wrong. Let me make a green tea. I have a whole day of writing ahead of me. I can't afford to be tired."

Fortunately, I have learned to trust the **Present Moment**, including my body's wise communication system. Rather than reaching for caffeine, masking the symptom (feeling tired), I went to my **Source** - **Stillness** - where true healing takes place. Sitting at my desk, I relaxed into my breath, dropped my palms to my lap, closed my eyes, and let go of any and all agenda including this writing or even the need to feel revitalized. Rather than fighting this tiredness, I simply sank into the truth of the moment.

Like an ocean wave receding back into the sea after having extended itself to the shoreline, I felt like I was sinking deeper and deeper into the tiredness. I stayed with my breath as I relaxed into the heavy feeling with a **Still** body and mind. After a few minutes, my eyes naturally opened and I began writing again, refreshed and awake. This is one out of hundreds of examples I have, demonstrating how sincere **Stillness** heals and revives one's energy when we allow it to do so.

STILLNESS HEALS AND ILLUMINATES NATURAL ENERGY

Now, for *"I"*: Illuminates. In the same way that **Stillness** heals, bringing one's energy entirely back to the body, it also illuminates that energy by freely shining it out from within. When we are caught in incessant doing and thinking, we lose access to the light within. Thoughts and anxious activity are like a shroud tossed over a lamp. Even though the light still shines, the mental chatter blocks it out, making it impossible to feel radiant, centered, and connected.

In our deepest state, *Inner Stillness*, we effortlessly shine, beaming from the overflow of energy circulating within us. There is nothing to do to create it. It is the *Source* of life itself. This inner light can make it's way out of our eyes, our presence, our voice, and our skin when we are relaxed, healthy, and at *home* in ourselves rather than lost in thought or enervating dramas. It is really quite simple. The more relaxed and present your are, the more you shine.

STILLNESS HEALS AND ILLUMINATES
NATURAL ENERGY

The final two letters in SHINE group together. "NE": Natural Energy. The very energy that fuels, heals, and shines through us is absolutely natural and infinite in supply. In the same way that one candle does not lose anything from lighting twenty more candles, this natural energy we are connected to is limitless and designed to effortlessly move through us. All we are asked to do is come into *Stillness* regularly and relax enough so that we can receive and transmit this energy in the same way a light bulb connects with electric energy and radiates light.

The purpose of this acronym and the SHINE Time practice is to offer you a simple path to allowing this infinite energy supply to create miracles in your life by bringing you back to your centered, whole, radiant *Diamond Self*... *here* and *now*. Not only does the practice of SHINE Time become as effortless as pausing to eat lunch when you are hungry, it also fuels your spirit, aligning you with more joy, inspiration, and radiant health.

Again, SHINE stands for *Stillness* Heals and Illuminates Natural *Energy*, recharging your body with energy, your mind with clarity, and creating a relaxed glow in your entire *Being*.

You ready to give it a try?

THE THREE B'S

The way to come into SHINE Time is through the Three B's. This is your sacred invitation to pause and "Be" with yourself in the heart of *Stillness*. First, make yourself comfortable, ideally in an uninterrupted space. With your eyes closed or softly open and still, focus your attention on the 3 B's:

1. BREATH
2. BODY
3. BROW CENTER

BREATH

Bring your breath into your body, bringing those lines of energy back in through the inhale and on the exhale letting go of any agendas and attachments.

BODY

Bring your **Awareness** to your body breathing, witnessing, and experiencing the expansion and contraction of your belly receiving the breath and releasing it on its own accord with the exhale. There is no doing here, just witnessing the Loving Intelligence beating your heart and moving your breath, as you rest with your attention on your body.

Listen to your body even deeper now. Without changing anything, simply notice where you may feel tense or heavy and what areas feel spacious and light. Silently and lovingly whisper to your body, *"I Am Here With You Now."*
I AM HERE.

Your body has likely been waiting a long time for this, for you, and for your attention. This mantra is very soothing and relaxing to the body. You may even choose to place one hand on your heart and one hand on your belly.

It is scientifically proven, that as mammals, we require physical warmth in order to feel safe and relaxed. By simply placing your own hands on your body, cortisol (the stress hormone) levels go down. This simple gesture of warmth and self-care is always available and transforms one's mindset, emotional well-being, and physical health over time. You can use this inner-embrace any time you seek solace and love. Personally, it is one of my sweetest daily habits and works every time. As you will see with practice, and maybe you already see, Presence and Self-Kindness have great power. Your loving attention is healing.

BROW CENTER

We have all heard the biblical reference, *"Let thine eye be single and thy whole body shall be filled with light."* What does this mean exactly? What was being referred to in that sacred statement?

In yogic teachings it is known that right between the eye brows is a powerful energy center called the Ajna Chakra, or what is most commonly known as the "third eye." This center is the seat of intuition, a deeper wisdom that is beyond what meets your physical eyes and certainly beyond the rational, thinking mind. Attuning to this center has countless benefits.

With your eyes closed, gently draw your gaze up to your brow center, or third eye... the space between your eye brows. If that is uncomfortable, direct your softly-closed eyes to the tip of your nose. The primary purpose of this is to bring your eyes to *stillness*. In Sanskrit, this is called a *dristi*, or focal point. When we have one-pointed focus, the mind also follows with a soothing centeredness. In focusing on the brow center, specifically, we balance the right and left hemispheres of the brain, while activating natural energy and awakening a higher level of consciousness.

Once you have dialed in the Three B's, **breathing** into the **body** as your eyes fall soft on the **brow** center, I invite you to place one hand on your heart and one hand on your belly. When you do this, you assimilate energy, power, and breath even more deeply into your own **Being**, while deepening this body connection. If you notice your mind and thoughts start to wonder, congratulations, you are human! Rather than fighting it, be gentle. Ease opens up as you witness and allow the mental chatter while directing your attention to your body breathing.

Remember, this is not about being perfect, but about having the courage to really see and be with yourself, building an inner-friendship that's free of judgment while being filled with loyalty and care. This simple practice of SHINE Time is the diamond doorway to awakening into the **Now**. Once you let go of the habit of running away from what you **think** is wrong with you or a feeling that may be uncomfortable, you gradually and wonderfully bloom into being relaxed, fully-expressed, and whole. In other words, you awaken into who you **Truly Are**!

Allowing whatever is present... thoughts, emotions, and physical sensations... to move like clouds passing through the sky activates spiritual liberation. The key is to keep breathing with the body as it opens and expands with the inhale, and then contracts and closes with the exhale. That pivot of focus from thinking to feeling your breath and body, however subtle, opens the door to **Presence**.

Just like anything else, when feelings seem too big, or discomfort in the body limits your peace, it is helpful to remember that *"this too shall pass."* Your emotional, mental, and physical terrain will change like the seasons, yet your real response is to release resistance by staying with your breath, body awareness, and brow center for a short interval of time.

IN AND OUT
    With each inhale, receiving vitality
    With each exhale, letting go of control

Inhale Peace
Exhale Forgiveness
Inhale Love
Exhale Compassion
Inhale Spaciousness
Exhale Trust
Inhale Ease
Exhale Acceptance
Breathing in deeply
Relaxing completely

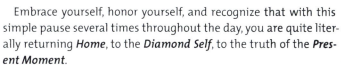

Embrace yourself, honor yourself, and recognize that with this simple pause several times throughout the day, you are quite literally returning *Home*, to the *Diamond Self*, to the truth of the *Present Moment*.

Your body, your breath, and the brow center are all here in this moment, which are entry points into the *Now*. As you drop into SHINE Time, you are awakening the *Diamond Self*. It is that simple and infinitely powerful.

You may be wondering how something so simple can be so powerful. The only way I can answer that question is with a metaphor. Imagine a gorgeous garden with flowers and singing birds, trees, fountains, and butterflies. In the center of this garden is an expansive 5-foot diamond statue. However beautiful, it may be a bit dusty or even caked with mud. Every time you come into SHINE Time, it is like washing pristine water over this priceless jewel, cleansing it, restoring it back to its original glow.

It is effortless. The more you relax, the easier this cleansing water flows over and around the gem. The deeper you breathe, the more fully the purifying water surges. The more courageously you embrace your body and feelings as they are, the brighter this diamond shines, and the more deeply you drop into your *Diamond Self*. Sometimes it may feel impossible to settle into the *Diamond Self*, or even connect in at all. The goal is not to be still and silent, for that agenda automatically rejects any noise or frenetic energy that may be very actively present. This is simply a practice of pausing and being fully awake and accepting of your body, mind, environment, and emotions as they are.

Unplugging from the day-to-day grind for regular segments of 2 minutes, 5 minutes, or even 20 minutes here and there has a transformational effect that grows over time. Research has proven that you can't break an old habit.

You can only create a new one, which activates a fresh neural pathway in the brain. The more you practice the new habit, the stronger that neural pathway becomes, gradually shifting you into a new reality with ease.

Rather than getting stressed or overwhelmed, which is simply a sign that you have gotten lost in doing, SHINE Time is one way to create a new neural pathway of peace and presence, empowering the *Diamond Self* to lead. Rather than living in the mind and visiting the *Present Moment* every now and then, the *Present Moment* becomes your primary residence where, more often than not, you naturally feel rested, stable, and grateful.

Regularly practiced in shorter increments, SHINE Time has the most lasting and beneficial impact. It becomes natural and familiar to pause every couple of hours, allowing peace to be your authentic set point. Eventually coming into SHINE Time happens naturally, as it did for me when I suddenly felt "tired" earlier as I was writing. The tiredness was my cue... to slow down and rest in the *Diamond Self*.

When I was a kid, my dad (being the great marathon runner that he was) would always say, *"slow and steady wins the race."* It was only recently that I began to grasp the profundity and comforting truth behind those words. The reality is, though, that there is no race (unless, of course, you are in a marathon) and the way to champion your way through life is by keeping with the essence of "slow and steady." With this approach to life, experiencing grace and ease in each moment becomes your set point, step by miraculous step.

SHINE TIME **WITH OPEN EYES**

SHINE Time is equally powerful when practiced with your eyes open. The pen in your hand, the flowers on your desk, the tree outside your window, the chair you are sitting on, a candle, or even a little freckle on the back of your hand; any or all of these can be used as a focal point that helps to migrate you from the thinking mind to the *Present Moment*. Anything that you can touch, see, taste, smell, or hear is a portal into *Being* and by keeping your eyes open, you can use what is right in front of you to awaken the treasure within.

The same process applies as when you have your eyes closed, focusing on the breath and body, only now you keep your eyes soft and still on one physical object or point in the room you choose to focus on. In the beginning, it is easiest to come into *stillness* and a silent mind while looking at the center of a flower or a candle flame. If you look at a pen, you may start reading the label, or an object that someone gave you may stimulate thinking about that person. The beauty of a flower is that it has no story. It simply is.

Much like the most beautiful things that life has to offer, discovering the treasure of life is quite simple, only requiring that you show up and choose to see, free of thought, what is tangibly with you now, in this moment. Every time you come back here you are quite literally polishing the diamond at the center of your **Being**, allowing your light to radiate with ease.

It's incredibly simple, I know. Just remember, this isn't about believing, this is about choosing to see and experience what unfolds for yourself. You can think of SHINE Time as an energy wash. Staying in the shower or having your hands under the faucet all day long is not the goal, but to simply rinse off regularly, revealing your natural energy *source* beneath the layers of chatter and rubble will leave you feeling refreshed, centered, and peaceful again and again.

STILLNESS
HEALS AND
ILLUMINATES
NATURAL
ENERGY

Stillness Heals and Illuminates Natural Energy

As I pause into this precious moment, **I AM** opening up to the love
and gentleness of my own heart. It feels good and natural to let go.
I AM allowing life to be as it is and I am allowing myself to be exactly as **I AM**.
I AM where I am meant to be now.
I AM breathing consciously into my ever-regenerating body.
My mind softens into Silence as I draw awareness to my brow center.
It feels sweet to be Present with myself.
I AM becoming my own best friend.
I love coming **Home** to the **Diamond Self** within. Living in the **Present Moment**
is natural for me and gets easier and easier each day.
I AM grateful to be here now!

SHINE!

If the only tool you utilize from this entire book is the practice of **SHINE TIME** in your everyday life, you are well on your way to experiencing this liberating transformation that you are choosing. May you plug into this natural energy supply, again and again, whenever you need it, knowing that the power is within you, accessible any time, any place. I celebrate you and honor the light within you. You are infinite!

Pause. Breathe Deeply. Fall in love with *Being*.

YOU ARE A DIAMOND!

PART TWO
TRANSFORMATIONAL JOURNEY

Chapter 7 - Awakening the Diamond Self – Week 1

Chapter 8 - Setting an Intention - Week 2

Chapter 9 - Awareness: Seeing Triggers as Treasures - Week 3

Chapter 10 - Using Medicinal Dialogue - Week 4

Chapter 11 - Making an Offering of Forgiveness to the Past - Week 5

Chapter 12 - Relaxing into Nothingness – Week 6

Chapter 13 - Declaring Your Destiny – Week 7

> *"This above all: 'to thine own self, be true."*
> William Shakespeare

Week One: Awakening The Diamond Self

For decades I betrayed the ever-available *Present Moment*, which was really a form of betraying myself, the *Diamond Self*, to solely focus on creating a future that I could finally relax or retire into. While I eventually arrived at what most would consider the perfect future, once I got there, I just couldn't settle into it. Even though my present was so good I was still finding problems to dwell on as I found myself lost in worry, upset, and discontent.

The same pain that pressed from within me when times were rocky pressed even harder when smooth sailing set in. Eventually, running on the "hamster wheel to nowhere" tired me out so much that I began to see, however hard the truth was to face, that I was the problem. No matter how good things were, I was the common denominator in the midst of it all, incapable of feeling peace within my wonderful life. I finally realized how perpetually lost I was in worry, upset, and doubt. My constant addiction to thinking about a better future or mulling over the past was the first step to awakening the **Diamond Self**. There is a point along the spiritual path where everything seems to get worse before it gets better. The darkest moment precedes the dawn. Typically, the triggers and challenges get so loud and persistent that the only thing left for anyone to do is to stop running, blaming, and fighting life and take a good look in the mirror. I had reached that place and little did I know then what a treasure that my falling apart would lead me to find.

The myth is that once we get the right gig, the right lover, the right house, the right body, the right clothes, and maybe even the weekly flower deliveries, it will be easy to live and love who we are. But, what if we get all of those things and still don't love ourselves very much, if at all... then what? What if what we think we are seeking never actually comes because what the soul is asking for can only be accessed right now at the center of our mess, at the core of what we don't want to acknowledge or accept?

THE SOUL'S CALL TO WAKE UP

At some point, no matter what your story is, you get the call to wake up to loving yourself deeply and completely... to putting your *True Self* above all else. Whether or not you answer the call is entirely up to you.

Often times, we avoid loving ourselves out of fear that putting ourselves first is selfish. Yet, once you take a good look at your life you will see how not putting yourself first creates instability, which not only leads to suffering, but to insecure relationships. It is no coincidence that flight attendants always instruct their passengers to secure their own oxygen mask in the face of a plane crash prior to securing their child's. This is a prime example that demonstrates how essential it is to love and tend to yourself first, even under the most dire circumstances.

Personally, when I am taking good care of myself, I feel alive and inspired, overflowing with enthusiasm and positive energy. The natural byproduct of feeling so deeply loved and safe within my own care is the desire to give with joy and kindness, free of expectations. When I feel good I want to surprise my beloved with a beautiful meal, sweet love notes, and maybe even a full-body massage. The feeling of generosity swells from within me when, first and foremost, I am being good to myself.

One of the most transformational choices that I've made along my journey into loving myself happened when I took the word "should" out of my vocabulary. For example,

"I **should** buy Christmas gifts."
"I **should** say 'yes' and go to that bridal shower."
"I **shouldn't** speak my truth to him or her."

Once I saw how toxic and confining following the book of etiquette was, I chose to drop the should's for good and simply lead my life with love and candor. The mind and ego has an agenda and expectations of how things "should" be or look, following the footprints of others. The heart, on the other hand, is dynamic, containing its own unique signature, and responds to each moment honestly and purely with no strings attached.

After a lifetime of being convinced that things should be handled a certain way and within a world of endless expectations, this can be challenging. It's because of this that for many, leaving "should" behind requires courage. Answering the soul call to awaken out of false conditions takes strength of heart and a deep connection to one's inner knowing. When you make the choice to love yourself above all else, it is likely that you will not fit the old mold anymore, which can make those who know you, and expect things of you, feel very uncomfortable. The good news is that once you understand this, it becomes easier to peacefully navigate through your soul's initial wake up call.

THE EGO'S RESISTANCE TO AWAKENING

The world and all of its super-sized options, deceiving advertisements, and shiny obsessions, coupled with those we love (and those we don't love) demanding we become something other than what we are, has created a sleepy society of people with overstuffed closets and emptied hearts. According to the world we live in, we learn which parts of ourselves we "should" accept and which parts "should" be buried completely out of sight. As early as five years old, we learn what actions will give us those shiny gold stars and what we need to change about ourselves, or worse to "fix," in order to ensure that we continue to stockpile more and more of those meaningless shiny stars of approval.

The bottom line is, we were born wild, free, and valuable, but over the course of living in a fearful world, we learn to pretend, hide, and hold our breath. As the prison doors screeched closed behind us, and the lock clicked into place, we finally, fully, and innocently became sheep. Bahhh!!! Okay, so I am being a bit dramatic here, but really it's more comedic than anything. We spend our lives masking ourselves. How? By focusing on things that we may have no genuine interest in, simply to ensure those colorful, shiny stars on our papers. Yet the reality of the situation is... ready??

WE ACTUALLY ARE THE STARS!

Well, it's worthy of a good body giggle, wouldn't you say? The truth is we are embodiments of light finding our way within a world of heavy "shoulds," where we learn to lug around cumbersome b.s. (belief systems) that were never ours to begin with. This is the societal norm.

Many people don't consciously realize they are burdened by "shoulds" and cultural "b.s.", yet the body is constantly communicating when a thought, expression, or action is out of personal integrity. Have you ever carried tension in your neck and shoulders? If so, look at the first six letters of the word "shoulder"... SHOULD. If you want to feel light again and relieve any shoulder tension, you may consider making a list of the things you do because you feel you should, or that you have to, or feel obligated to do. Notice as you take things off the list how your shoulders loosen and the energy returns to your body. The correlation amazed me when I first dug deep into that one. This is a simple, powerful way to loosen up, love yourself up, and liberate the *Diamond Self* from within you.

The truth is love is not conditional. *Love* is not attached to an outcome. Love could care less what kind of car you drive or how successful your marriage is. Love doesn't care if you fit in. It doesn't try to transform you into something better. It doesn't punish or judge. It doesn't bury parts of you or convince you that you have done something wrong... or right. Love is our *Home*. When we wake up to this Love, we create heaven on Earth, which is radically and wildly independent of all outer circumstances. *Home*... the house that never forecloses... the sanctuary within that is forever available to you, *Now*.

WHEN A HOMELESS MAN LED ME HOME

I will always remember this one particularly busy morning in Los Angeles. I had a list of five important errands in my hands with only one hour to run them all. It was a stretch, but I was on a mission. As I exited the market, the final stop of my errands, I was feeling efficient and even on time as I neared my car. An important meeting awaited me at *home*, so I was ready to race off to the rest of my day. Just a few feet away from my car, a *home*less man tried to stop me as he asked for some money for food.

I whizzed past him, paused briefly and then quickly fired off, *"Sorry, I'm in a rush."* His furious desperation stopped me in my tracks. *"Where in God's name is everyone going?! You are always running somewhere!"*

He was right. It wasn't just this particular day. It was **EVERYDAY!** Whether I was escaping a needy *home*less man, dodging a phone call, blowing through stop signs on the way to yoga class - the ultimate irony - or having my guard up with my beloved, I was a foreigner to what was right in front of me, and within me for that matter.

My keys accidentally dropped to the ground. Truth has gravity to it. As I reached for them and my wallet, my eyes softened as they focused on his.

"You are my teacher today. I was lost in a race to nowhere. Thank you for bringing me back."

My sudden shift into being fully attentive was as disarming to him as his words of truth were to me. His anger dropped as quickly as my keys. He rapidly offered a spontaneous, heartfelt apology.

"I didn't mean to hurt your feelings, Miss" he softened.

I waved it off as I handed him five bucks while we continued with a heart to heart conversation that floored both of us. As I hugged this teacher in disguise and got into my car, tears streamed down my face. I nodded as he bopped his heart a couple of times with a smile. It was a powerful moment, where we both walked away feeling stronger and more open than before our exchange.

From there, my entire day shifted. I was clearly established in **Presence**. I could feel my heart awake and alive. My eyes were on the road, taking in the trees that lined the streets as I drove along to my meeting. It didn't matter that I was a few minutes behind. The only thing not worth losing is my center and thanks to life loving me, as she loves all of us, I was able to find my way back *home* on the outstretched wings of a homeless man. Imagine if I would have let a "should" get in the way of that miracle.

"You know you shouldn't talk to homeless people. They are dirty and dangerous. You have to be right on time. You should be perfect. You should never be late."

I would have missed the sheer beauty that life presented, which only my present heart has the key to unlock.

Typically, within the day-to-day grind, we lose sight of the miracles of love that are everywhere. We become convinced that if we just win this one race, then everything will fall into place and we can finally relax. There's always time to love later, isn't there? We want to push and prove that we're brilliant, powerful, and worthy by achieving now, so we can feel loved, accepted, and maybe even worthy enough to go on vacation tomorrow. But, what if brilliance and self-worth have nothing to do with all you have accomplished, all you know, or how much faster you can run than the thousands who lag behind? What if freedom and peace were your measuring sticks for success? The **Present Moment** is the only point in time that actually exists and the only way you will ever find the sense of **Home** you seek?

As the homeless man so clearly showed me, what if being at **home** has nothing to do with having a roof over my head and everything to do with being present and fully engaged with what is right in front of me right now?

THE FIVE ATTRIBUTES OF THE DIAMOND SELF

Obviously, it required some degree of **Presence** for me to even recognize the opportunity that was presented through the **home**less man in the parking lot that day. I often wonder how many miracles I must have missed out on prior to my journey into awakening the **Diamond Self** and how many enchanting experiences I now get to enjoy thanks to my ever-blooming devotion to this very moment. This one. This moment. Right now, as I write these words.

In order to awaken the **Diamond Self**, there are five attributes or qualities to embrace that all conveniently begin with the letter "A" to help you migrate from the slumber of the mind and ego, to the marvelous, sparkling alertness of your **True Self**. These five attributes serve as a clear map that make it easy to mine these gems from within the everyday challenges as they present themselves... breaking through them rather than being broken by them.

Challenges are really gifts in disguise. The reality is that life will continue to offer you these opportunities until the particular lesson that your soul is undergoing is learned. Once we take responsibility and begin to tend to ourselves within, we stop blaming others for feeling like life is against us when things are not working the way we want them to. Through this action we activate true power. It certainly is the path less traveled, which is why so few people are genuinely empowered, joyful, and free.

The liberating news is that if you are feeling it, then the emotion lives inside of **you**. Now make it your sacred mission to shift from obsessing over the trigger to powerfully living the treasure, which is the transformation that this book is designed to help you through. This shift immediately moves you from the victim of circumstance to the victorious champion of your valuable, precious life.

Once I started embodying these five attributes, I began to realize that life was not happening to me, but is always happening *for* me and my soul's highest purpose. Can you imagine the joy that sets in when you realize how powerful you are and that your freedom and peace of mind have nothing to do with outer circumstances? In the following chapters, we will go deeper into the 5 A's of the *Diamond Self*. For now, here is a brief overview.

ATTRIBUTE #1: AWARENESS

Simply stated, *Awareness* is a state of mind that allows you to see life as it is, clearly and non-judgmentally, with your senses keen, bright, and awake. If *Presence* is a state of being, *Awareness* is a state of mind that allows you to bloom into being. *Awareness* is a shift to the five senses in which you fully experience what is right in front of you. Anything you can see, hear, taste, smell, and touch is part of the *Present Moment*. Rather than thinking about life, the *Diamond Self* is aware, witnessing what is tangible in the Now and even witnessing the thinking mind with spacious *Presence*. Coming to your senses and observing without identification is the easiest way to activate this pure state of mind.

The third step of the *Diamond Process* is entirely devoted to *Awareness*, which is covered in greater depth in chapter nine.

ATTRIBUTE #2: AUTHENTICITY

The second attribute of the *Diamond Self* is *Authenticity*, the key to freedom. Rather than discriminating between what you should or shouldn't say, or what is right or wrong, you align with the *Diamond Self* by expressing feelings openly, responsibly, and fully as they arise, within your own Space of Love (which we will soon go over) or with someone you trust. When the "shoulds" and "should nots" are dropped, and all that is left is a candid response to each individual moment of life, you are living as your *Diamond Self*.

ATTRIBUTE #3: ALLOWANCE

Allowance is the power of letting life be as it is and trusting in it's Divine perfection. By honoring life's full circle as something greater than what you can see or understand from your partial perspective as an individual, you grow closer to the *Diamond Self*.

When you see the dance between opposites, creation and destruction... negative and positive, as equally essential to evolution and expansion, fragmenting opinions tend to soften. By allowing all things to exist as they are with the wisdom that what we resist persists, the *Diamond Self* blooms. This doesn't exclude discernment or taking action to protect yourself or someone else when needed. This is simply a recognition that everything is always happening in perfect order, no matter how chaotic things may seem. Rather than getting lost in fighting what is, you always have the power to trust the innate worth of each unique facet upon the gem of *Life*.

ATTRIBUTE #4: ACCEPTANCE

Awakening the *Diamond Self* means allowing the moment to be as it is and accepting responsibility that the reality you find yourself in is part of your own creation. Ew! I know that can be a tall order and yet, in practice the rewards are endless.

From this perspective, anything can arise while a deep trust remains that everything is conspiring for your growth, evolution, and liberation. You have the power to see life and each moment in it as though your soul had chosen the events. When there is no obstruction to what is, this is the attribute that leads to total freedom. The attribute of Acceptance also requires that you discover and own all different sides of your personality, or what I refer to as "facets."

Funny

Sexy

Fierce

Vulnerable

Wise

Jealous

Peaceful

Greedy

Generous

Introverted

Bitchy

Pure

Poetic

Exuberant

Is it possible that you are everything? Accepting yourself entirely allows the whole *Diamond*, with all of her facets, to shine from within you, freeing hidden gifts that are unique to your design, while actualizing your full potential.

ATTRIBUTE #5: APPRECIATION

Just as one would regularly water a seed within a garden, what you appreciate in your life grows. Having an attitude of gratitude and consciously taking time to give thanks for what you have is one of the most instantaneous ways of uplifting your state of mind and **Being**.

When you can learn to appreciate challenges as opportunities for growth and awakened consciousness, rigidness melts away, making space to see through the eyes of the **Diamond Self**. This one attribute for awakening the **Diamond Self**, in and of itself, has great alchemical power that transforms you from seeing life as hard or even unbearable to a joyful adventure of love, expansion, and endless support. **Appreciation** is a super power!

Stillness Heals and Illuminates Natural Energy

    I invite you to completely drop everything that you've just read, trusting that whatever is in your highest good is already integrated and available when you need it. Relax your jaw, loosen your belly, soften your hips and shoulders, and simply breathe consciously into your body, bringing full awareness and energy back to yourself. For the next couple of minutes, feel free to close your eyes and empower the 3 B's: Breath, Body Awareness, Brow Center. Remember, your body benefits greatly and relaxes when you consciously breathe into it and are Present with it. Explore for yourself and when you feel complete, open your eyes and enjoy the following practice.

Your Gem Power Declaration

I trust this moment. I trust myself. Life loves me and is conspiring for my Highest Good here, now, and always.

Diamond Self Activation
Putting it into Practice...

I. CREATE AND SIT IN YOUR SPACE OF LOVE:

As Joseph Campbell says, *"your sacred space is where you can find yourself again and again."* Your Space of Love is your sanctuary where you return to yourself. It is created by you and for you to sit in daily where there are no decisions to be made, and no distractions to overcome. It's simply spaciousness for you to explore and relax into. It used to be most common for spiritual seekers to leave all of their possessions behind to go meditate in a cave. In today's world, a new model of awakening is on the rise, empowering you to embody the light of your **Diamond Self** as you remain in the world. The easiest way to do this is to sit regularly in silence as you connect to the deeper truth within. Sitting in your Space of Love makes it easier for you to remain centered through the inevitable ups and downs that are part of your life.

Your Space of Love can be as simple as having a pillow to sit on and one candle on a low table in a private corner of your **home**, or it can be as elaborate as having an entire, technology-free room devoted to your spiritual practices and **SHINE Time**. The key is to find someplace in your **home** that is quiet and private where you can place a few objects that represent the **Diamond Self** and inspire your cultivation of centering into **Presence**.

I keep what I love the most in my Space of Love: images of spiritual masters, statues of radiant deities, candles, fresh flowers, inspiring books, essential oils, incense, and even my sacred Runes that were my first spiritual purchase at nineteen years old. At any given moment I can sit in my Space of Love and be present with a flower as I deepen in my breath and senses. It's here where I trade worries and to-do lists for the stillness of the **Present Moment**, while being surrounded by reflections of peace and beauty.

Spaciousness. Simplicity. Stillness. Silence. These are the qualities you want to keep close to heart when choosing a location for and creating your Space of Love.

In order to take time out in your Space of Love, setting healthy boundaries will be highly supportive and allow you to get the most out of this book. For example, you may let your family know that you will be taking some time out for yourself and ask that they respect your needs for privacy during the times you request. You may also shift your work schedule so that you have the mornings and/or evenings free of technology so you can deepen in **SHINE Time** without concern for others' expectations. When you choose to trade multitasking and draining influences for loving focus and self-care, then you will get the most out of this book and the practices within it.

One inspiring truth to keep close to heart: When you say *"no"* to what you don't want, you are simultaneously saying *"yes"* to wellbeing and what you do want.

II. CREATE YOUR JOY MAP:

Being in the **Present Moment** is easy when you are focused on what brings you joy. Since over-thinking is what leads to suffering, and being **Present** is what leads to prospering, the question becomes *"what brings you into the Present Moment?"* Creating a **Joy Map** is one lovely way of living the answer to that empowering question.

Open your journal to a blank page. In the middle of the page, draw a heart (a diamond symbol or circle shape will also work). At the center of the heart, label your **Joy Map** with your name. For example, mine reads "Veronica's **Joy Map**." From the outer edges of the heart, draw spokes to the edge of the page. On each spoke, write one item that makes you feel good and brings you joy. In other words, write down something that softens and brings ease and brightness to your heart. You can have as many spokes and items as you want on this one page, stemming from the symbol at the center.

In my own journal I have a colorful *Joy Map* page that's filled with items and experiences I love such as using essential oils, arranging flowers around my *home*, being present with my kitty cat while she is purring, walking and jogging in nature, making YouTube videos, being with trees and animals, visioning my dream *home*, singing mantras and hymns, dressing up and using fashion as a form of art and personal expression, swimming in the natural water of a lake, river or the ocean, receiving a massage, doing random acts of kindness, practicing yoga, meditating, having a technology-free day, reading an inspiring book, and dancing.

You can keep this *Joy Map* in your Space of Love and update it as you discover more and more of the things in life that you love. Once your *Joy Map* is created, circle one item that speaks to you the most and indulge in it this week, making the empowerment of joy a weekly habit.

III. SELF-NURTURING PRACTICE:

It is highly beneficial to tend to all four areas of yourself (spiritual, mental, emotional, and physical) by adding in high vibrational elements to your life while also clearing away what no longer serves your highest good. For example, you may consider clearing stressors such as clutter, cutting out unhealthy relationships, setting healthy boundaries, simplifying your diet, reading inspiring books, reducing social media, increasing time in nature (or playing with your pet or child), walking with a friend you feel peaceful around, or practicing yoga and meditation. The key to a practice of transformational self-nurturing is to remember these 3 things.

* Tend to each of the four levels of being:
mental, emotional, physical, spiritual

* Focus on your joy vs. what your mind thinks it "should" do. A clarifying question to ask yourself is, "What makes me feel alive?" For example, your mind may say "join a gym" while your heart's desire is to walk in nature, jump on a trampoline, or attend dance classes. Follow your unique bliss.

* Less is more. You can always do more if you feel the inspiration to. When you only commit to what you can definitely do and follow through with your manageable agreement, you are building self-trust. Again *"slow and steady wins the race."*
Remember to be specific concerning how much time each day, and how many times per week you are committing to each practice. For example: Under the Emotional level of being, you may commit to freely dancing to your

favorite song (5 mins) 2 x's this week. Under the Physical level of being, you may commit to drinking two green smoothies or green juices this week. I suggest creating a Weekly Self-Nurturing Tracking Sheet like the one on the next page and post it up somewhere you will see it daily. Simply, write your goals in the "weekly commitment" section and then check off what you have done each day.

DIAMOND SELF ACTIVATION (JOURNAL QUESTIONS)

* What stops you from being Present or taking time out of your day for stillness and self-care?

* How do you sense that you will benefit from opening more to the *Present Moment*?

* How do you feel about creating your Space of Love and prioritizing pockets of silence, *Presence*, and spaciousness for yourself over the next week?

* How many times this week, and for how long, will you practice SHINE Time? The key here is to be specific (i.e. 2 days this week for 20 minutes). Remember, less is more. If you do more, great, but the main thing is to only commit to what you can definitely follow-through with, as this creates *Self-Trust* and congruence.

Diamond Self-Nurturing Sheet

Weekly Commitment:	Physical	Emotional	Mental	Spiritual
Monday				
Tuesday				
Wednesday				
Thursday				
Friday				
Saturday				
Sunday				

> *"Your vision becomes clear when **you look into your heart**.*
> *Who looks outside, dreams.*
> *Who looks inside, awakens."*
> *Carl Jung*

Week Two: Setting An Intention

Have you ever wondered about the Universe, Creator, God, Goddess, Spirit, the Loving Intelligence, the Tao... the Life-Giving Energy that creates and sustains worlds? There are countless names for this **Great Mystery**. Yet we continue to wonder about the nature of this undeniable **Magnificent Presence** that moves through **all** of us, and all of Life, as it pushes clouds through the skies, lifts blades of grass from beneath the dark, coarse soil towards the light, and creates an infinite number of one-of-a-kind expressions of life... from snowflakes, to flowers, to the creatures of the land and sea.

What is this **Abundant Magnificence** that keeps the sun blazing, the stars sparkling, and the tides turning, not to mention, our hearts beating and our breath endlessly cycling in and out without an ounce of effort on our parts? Clearly it's something other than our own exhaustive doingness... the dripping of our own blood, sweat, and tears... that provides and sustains **Life**. While we have all experienced this invisible force, what we may sometimes forget is that It has nothing to do with our own will. It has moved through life way before we arrived and will continue on eternally, well beyond our inevitable departures.

No matter how many check marks on your "to do list," something other than the churning of your own wheel is at work, as *It* devotedly heals scraped knees, races to mend broken bones, and stabilizes the beating of our hearts. It does this continuously, bringing regeneration where it is needed with loyalty, purity, and precision. The questions that I ask you now are:

"Do you trust this mysterious force enough to call upon it and relax into it?"
"Do you trust it's reliability and loyalty?"
"Most especially, do you trust it's loyalty to YOU?"

THE POWER OF CHOICE

Day in and day out, we make choices, from what to eat and wear to work, to what we read and who we invest our energy with. As soon as we make the choice and focus, that very mysterious life force fuels the very thing that our attention is focused on. Choices happen all the time. The challenge is that most of those choices simply happen by default as we unconsciously repeat a pattern that was often learned from limited people within less than ideal situations.

The opportunity we all have is to begin designing our lives intentionally and purposefully from our own intuition and heart-centered internal guidance. For example, you may be working in a job that you hate, assuming that it is what you "have" to do. If this is your situation, as it is for many, you may consider choosing a new perspecitve that can free your dreams from a limited mindset.

Perhaps, you witnessed your own mother or father struggling through an exhausting career and for some reason find yourself in a very similar pattern. Whether you know it or not, you are a powerful co-creator and worthy of living the outcome of your heart's desire. With this in mind, the questions to ask yourself are:

"What is my heart's intention?" and
"What inspiring new way do I choose to activate and empower with my focused, loving attention?"

THE EVOLUTIONARY IMPULSE

Life is self-perfecting with expansion continuously taking place. One of nature's laws is that it's designed to bloom and thrive. Unlike the rest of the natural world, you have the ability to consciously know yourself, and to see where you are stuck, so that you can correct your own course as you choose, instead, and evolve. What a super power! Have you ever contemplated this? Every other animal in the natural world responds to the *Present Moment* as it is, free of thinking, through instinct alone. On the other hand, we humans are actually aware - sometimes acutely - of ourselves. We can race our consciousness way outside of ourselves and watch, as if witnessing from an outsider's perspective. We can see the big picture from above, only we are not above, but are smack in the middle of the situation.

While in previous chapters I have emphasized the power of *Presence* and stilling the mind, now we get to look at how we can consciously use our minds to evolve and awaken into greater Love. For a moment let's begin by considering the animal kingdom. Do you think that a bunny rabbit is consciously aware that it is a bunny rabbit within a whole, diverse, wildly magnificent system? The bunny rabbit just is. It is simply responding to life by instinct in each moment, free of mental chatter (which... okay... I admit, this is something that I sometimes envy).

When the bunny is hungry, it seeks food; when it senses danger, it runs; when it yearns to procreate, it hops onto one of its many fluffy lovers. (Perhaps this is another reason to envy those adorable creatures, but hey, I digress!) The point I am making here is that there is no thinking, judging, or opinion involved on the part of the bunny... just instinct. This is the beauty of nature. Without mental chatter and filled with natural expression, nature lives in peace. This is why our darkest moments often drive us to sit in the forest or by the ocean. Nature and Silent *Presence* heals.

However, in contrast, doesn't it sometimes seem as though we were given the gifts of self-awareness and thought as forms of punishment or torture? I only ask because many, including me, have at one point or another found ourselves loathsome of our humanness. Why? Many times the thinking mind seems to be our greatest obstacle to peace. Could it possibly be that it was a mistake or some form of impediment within the chain of evolution? Let me ask you this... the same question that I must also ask myself... Do you really think that this incredible Loving Intelligence, the same one that miraculously heals a scraped knee again and again and again, makes mistakes? Do you think - "think" being the key word here - that thinking needs to be cured or silenced?

There are countless practices designed to kill the ego and silence the mind. Although stillness and silence are key attributes of our **True Nature**, the power of the mind is simultaneously our unique gift! It is the ultimate paradox. When and if it's used wisely, the poison, so to speak, can also be the remedy. We have the ability to direct this **Loving Intelligence** toward creating what we love by using the mind to envision our heart's calling. In the same way that the human body directs this force to heal, correct, and perfect itself, we can mentally program it to empower our dreams and increase our spiritual evolution, if we desire to do so.

YOU ARE A ONE-OF-A-KIND DESIGN!

What if you knew that your heart-centered dreams, and all that you truly love, were planted within you in the same way that a mango tree is encoded with its own unique design? When provided with the proper conditions, like sunshine, water, and rich soil, this tree produces a very nourishing, most luscious, and abundant harvest.

What if your unique design was an essential component of the Whole? What if, just like the gardener who spends her time planting crops in rich soil beneath the life-giving sun, then patiently tends to them with water and care, your own task was to discover the seed planted within you and tend to it with devotion?

As I shared in chapter five, our Inner Purpose is to awaken the **Diamond Self**... that pure source of Light and **Presence** within which stands like a pillar, unchanging and powerful. Yet, our Outer Purpose, as we'll fully dive into in Part Four of this book, evolves over time, and has everything to do with our unique talents, life experience, and joyful heart-centered desires.

On one hand, realizing one's unique potential planted deep within one's human design can be wonderfully inspiring. Yet on the other, the ego can come up with a million excuses as to why one should stay locked in a cubicle, far from the sun, where harsh, predictable supervision prevents the seed from sprouting. However, the **Diamond Self** only knows perfection, and trusts that even feeling stuck in an undesirable situation, however far from glorious it may feel at times, is part of the soul's journey.

Being lost and locked is the first step to being found and free. Quantum physicists have discovered, even on a molecular level, that order follows chaos. In the same way, if you are feeling confused and unclear about what to do with your life, realize that this is the precursor of your return to clarity and a sense of purpose. Life is an eternal dance between opposites and making peace with both ends of the spectrum is the way to enjoy your ever-evolving journey. Being Present helps us to open up and accept what is. The power of intention provokes the fruition of what we choose.

When we realize that we, as humans, have the ability to influence the *Infinite Intelligence* that animates all of life, the whole game changes and a new possibility opens up. When we couple clear vision with the embodied thriving **Presence** that nature models for us, we become magicians who are capable of inspiring greatness, and transforming thought energy into matter, as we invoke who we were designed to become.

Yet sadly most of us are so preoccupied with battling and surviving that we end up unconsciously creating more for ourselves to battle. Anyone who has broken out of a troubling reality into something wonderful will tell you that it began with an understanding of what no longer served them, followed by a crystal clarity concerning their most passionate desires.

WHAT IS INTENTION?

Intention is a form of input that informs and directs the Loving Intelligence to move in a certain direction. This organizing intelligence responds to your emotional and mental input every time you consciously or unconsciously feel, think, or declare something. You can think of intention as the address or destination that you plug into your car's navigation system. Your emotions and thoughts are driving and influencing the organizing intelligence at all times. Cooperative elements attract and arrange themselves according to your state of being and intention, conscious or otherwise. So, the real questions for you now are:

"What is the direction of your sails and rudder?"
*"Have you found your **North Star**?"*

There are endless intentions you can set for specific events or chapters within your day. For instance, setting an intention each morning is a powerful way to direct your day consciously and positively. Many years ago, I remember walking into the bathroom early one morning and discovering my boyfriend at the time sitting in a chair with his eyes closed, deep in focused thought, smiling and joyfully muttering to himself. As it turns out, that morning I learned one of his secrets to his grand level of success in the world.

Each morning as soon as he woke up, his ritual was to play the events of the day in his mind's eye just as he would like to see it go. More importantly, he did so with feeling and detail. This was something that he'd been doing naturally since he was five or six years old, and had worked in miraculous ways throughout his entire life. As a child, he was impoverished and beaten up at school on a daily basis, so he resorted to his imagination to create a vision where he was the triumphant star. By using this technique he was also able to give back to others in need, which is exactly what he does to this day.

He so deeply enjoyed escaping into his imagination with such loyalty and trust that what he imagined eventually came true. The mind does not know the difference between imagined and real. This is why you can imagine a terrible thought and suddenly feel your heart begin to pound and a queasiness in your stomach, even though what you are imagining is not a real event. Our thoughts contain more power than we have been taught to realize. When you become intentional about where you direct your mental and emotional energy, you begin to experience your life as art. Much like Michelangelo co-creating, "The David," in collaboration with Spirit you become the co-sculptor of your life.

WHAT IS A SCENE INTENTION?

Just like a play that's been written with a number of various scenes, your day consists of many individual scenes that we know as moments. Any time that you move about, either to a new location or a different activity, you are switching scenes in your life's daily story. Another way for you to utilize intention is by directing your intentions concerning specific scenes of your life, which can range all the way from the mundane to major life experiences. For example, I often like to use intention to manifest the perfect parking spot. Prior to arriving at my destination, I usually imagine a couple of spots open as I pull straight into one of them, or a car pulling out just as I am driving up. When people ride along with me, they often say *"Wow! You have a parking fairy on your side."* Yep! And that fairy's name is **intention**.

You can also set a scene intention to nail a job interview, feel confident and present on a first date, or even for safety and ease before getting in the car. One of my favorites is to set a bedtime scene intention just before I drift off to sleep. Research shows that what you are focused on just before you go to sleep not only affects your dream state, but also determines how you will wake up. Every night before bed I say, "My intention is to sleep soundly in service to waking up refreshed, restored, and rejuvenated." Sometimes, I add in a second intention to let go of any weakening judgments that I may have placed on myself or others that day. In this way, my intention works to cleanse out and detoxify my mental body.

An easy way to create an intention is to ask yourself what quality you would like to have more of during that specific scene, your day, or overall in your life. For example, if you would like to feel more clarity and calm, you can set the intention *"My intention is to embody clarity and serenity today with ease and grace"* I always like to add the words "ease and grace" into my intentions to align with the most graceful route to my "destination".

Some of my favorite morning and bedtime intentions:

MORNING INTENTIONS:
My intention is to serve as a beneficial presence today with ease and grace.
My intention is to embody the deepest level of Presence with ease, grace, and freedom.
My intention is to be an instrument of prosperity, appreciation, and love today.

BEDTIME INTENTIONS:
My intention is to heal at the deepest level available to me with ease and grace.
My intention is to clear any and all negative judgments I have placed on myself and others today.
My intention is to be divinely guided and protected while I sleep.
My intention is to sleep soundly tonight in service to waking up in the morning refreshed, restored, and rejuvenated.

WHAT IS NORTH STAR INTENTION?

As you can see, intention keeps you focused on what you want, by guiding your ship and using the inevitable winds of change to fill your sails, towards your heart's core purpose. This is what I refer to as your **North Star**. Your **North Star** is a clear, singular vision that you use to continuously bring yourself back on course in order to powerfully move forward.

If we are divided with several visions, we get lost in confusion and frustration. With that said, it is highly beneficial to attune your heart to the overall purpose of your life by clarifying your **North Star Intention**. This is the quality that you keep coming back to, which ensures that you stay on track with what truly matters to you most. This is your opportunity to get ultra clear on *why* you want what you want.

The beloved Sadguru Shankaracharya, a living master in Boulder, Colorado, helped me

to look at **why** I do, say, and believe what I do. He taught me to become diligent with this form of self-inquiry. The reason that it's important to clarify the "why" is to make sure that your intention is one that is pure and that comes genuinely from your heart rather than coming from the inflated ego's idea of right and wrong. If you choose to awaken the treasure within you, leading from your heart, versus your ego and mind, becomes your greatest priority.

Personally, my **North Star Intention** is to embody the deepest level of **Presence** available to me. Through the years, I have noticed that as soon as I set this intention, I migrate from my mind to the moment and from that place I make myself available to the highest possibility. I use this intention before client sessions, speaking engagements, or sweet moments with my beloved. When I am Present, I feel at Home, which allows me to relax into and enjoy the sweetness of life.

What destination are you making your way towards, step by step, moment by moment, each and every day? "What are you choosing to blossom into more and more every day?" Whatever that quality is, just know that what you seek is not outside of you in the future. It lives within you Now and through your **North Star Intention** you can remove whatever has stood in the way of your full potential to invoke what you truly love again and again.

EMBODY THE VIBRATION OF YOUR RADIANT VISION

If you don't know where you want to be, yet you are very dissatisfied with where you are- the good news is knowing what you don't want is helping you get crystal clear on what you do want. On the other hand, we have all heard that you attract what you are - what you think and feel. So, if you are dwelling on how terrible your life's conditions are, this only brings you more of the same. This is why coming Home, beyond the worry, doubt, and upset, to your True Self, the **Diamond Self**, is essential, as it empowers you to vibrate **with** your vision instead.

I remember a time in my life when my financial world had been turned completely upside down. I was devastated financially and because of this I kept focusing my intentions on having more money. After a couple of years of this grueling financial struggle, I began to give up on the power of intention, and instead became frustrated and angry, which was actually my first step in the right direction. Remember, **authenticity** is one of the key attributes of the **Diamond Self**.

As I dug deeper, I realized it was not money that I wanted, but **Freedom**. I felt trapped, powerless, and stuck. Instead what I wanted was to feel empowered and able to move around in my life in the way that I was inspired to.

Once I'd clarified the quality at the core of the "thing" that I thought I wanted (Freedom), rather than wallowing in lack I began asking myself constructive questions like "what would make me feel free and abundant right now?"

The two main answers that I received were, 1) enjoying more time relaxing outdoors, and 2) getting massages. From that point on, I made a commitment to rest each day under my favorite tree and each night before bed to give myself foot massages with coconut oil. Interestingly enough, during that time I started to flower into deeper levels of **Presence**, both with my body through the foot massages, and with **Nature** during my regular **Diamond Dates** at the park. As a result, my energy began to climb as I focused on the beauty that was right in front of me instead of continuing in the draining habit of worry and upset due to my self pity. And wouldn't you know, but this was when a financial solution finally came bounding into my life as well.

I realized then that the highest possibilities arise from the midst of the silence... out of **Presence**. It will never come from a busy, overwhelmed, or over-thinking mind. This was when my own **North Star Intention** birthed: *My intention is to embody the deepest level of Presence available to me now.* I come back to this again and again any time that I feel scattered, drained, or upset. So long as I am Present, I feel peacefully alive and resourceful, even in the face of challenges, and my life flows from there.

When we are in the **Diamond Self**, we drop out of the unconscious spinning cycle of fear-based thinking and into deep appreciation, surrender, and faith.

This allows the **Loving Intelligence** to move the highest possibility through us and our lives. Trusting the **Loving Intelligence** is simple from the **Diamond Self**'s perspective because when we are dialed into the moment, we are naturally embodying the peace, harmony, and wisdom that we are calling upon.

It is predominantly limited and negative thinking that creates suffering. If I would have remained stuck on not having enough money, I would have become even more lost and drained. The mind is like a maze. On the other hand, the heart is more of a labyrinth. The difference is that a maze has endless blocks and confusing entrances and exits, while a labyrinth has only one way in and one way out. When we lead with **Presence** and **Love**, our lives pulse with clarity, aliveness, and serenity. This is why it is essential to slide into the home base of the **Diamond Self**, again and again, as a means of migrating from the maze of the mind into the magical labyrinth of the heart's wisdom. This is the one place where the voice of the soul can be heard... and followed.

THE POWER OF APPRECIATION

One of the five attributes of the **Diamond Self** is **Appreciation**, which is the awareness and enjoyment of things and people, yourself included. Purely and simply, if you appreciate the things that are working in your life, you get more to appreciate. Conversely, if you dwell on what is not working, you get more struggle and strife. Have you ever noticed that?

To take it a step further, rather than dismissing the strife and pretending it is not there, as you will see in the next chapter, there is a grand treasure within those triggers. The first step to use in uncovering the treasure during times of challenge is to ask the expansive question, "What is this situation trying to teach me?" It will always lead to a more constructive - maybe even appreciative - mind pattern, as opposed to destructively wallowing in the notion that life is hard.

As you can see from my previous story, struggling financially for an extended period of time brought me something infinitely more valuable and lasting. How could I not appreciate the trigger? It not only led me to deepening in **Self-Care** and **Presence**, it also led me to a much more empowered way of earning, investing, and handling money. The more we look for the message in the mess, and move with **Appreciation**, the greater the Universe responds with gifts to appreciate. The **Organizing Intelligence** is not personal, but one way or another it is quite generous in how loyally it responds to our thoughts and feelings.

THE POWER OF ASKING FOR WHAT YOU NEED

Part of empowering your full potential is not only about clarifying your heart-felt intention, it also involves **asking** for what you need clearly, lovingly, and **free of attachment**. Ew! That last part can be especially challenging for some of us - free of attachment.

Today, we are seeing the repercussions of a culture not asking for what they want in a clear, loving manner, and without attachment, within the epidemic we know as divorce. As we know, approximately 50% of first marriages end in divorce in the U.S. Within second and third marriages, the percentage increases. Why are these rates so high? A large part of this telling number comes down to lack of communication.

The reality is that we live in a culture that typically reacts rather than communicates, while expecting others to know their needs rather than clearly and lovingly expressing what is needed. As I began awakening to my full potential and the *Diamond Self*, it became inevitable that I'd learn to speak my truth, and have the courage to ask that my needs be met, regardless of how the person responded. What I discovered in this process was that I had a habit of expecting my loved ones to know what I needed. As a result, when I didn't receive what was so important to me, I'd get angry and become distant with them, even though they had no idea about any of my needs to begin with. How could they? I hadn't told them a thing. That's the funny thing about mind reading... it never seems to work.

Typically, when there is upset inside, the fight or flight response kicks in, keeping the person locked in an unconscious, unloving pattern. Fortunately, there is an alternative to fight or flight, which we will discuss in the next chapter. For now, it is important to note the significance of becoming stellar at *asking for what you need* as you let go of *any* attachment to the outcome.

Prior to developing their mental capacity, children are pre-cognitive and neurologically don't know how to ask for what they need just yet. They communicate with emotions rather than words. In order to get attention and hopefully receive what he/she needs, the child will typically throw a tantrum. Once there is enough noise, the parent will likely go over and address the child. For most children, this habit continues into adulthood, making this limited style of communication a habit. Thus the individual learns early on that by getting upset attention will be given, which was the original desire. However, the problem is that turmoil and tantrums become woven into one's relationships, which make for rocky, unsettled relationship foundations.

Not asking clearly and lovingly while expecting your needs to be met is the source of most pain and fighting in relationships, not to mention war on a national and international scale. In order to align with your full potential, and thus lead an empowered life, it's essential for you to discover what you need and get really good at responsibly asking for it, free of any attachment. Asking for what you need is the first step to receiving. Without being stellar at asking, you risk getting lost in what you definitely don't want and feeling frustrated, resentful, and powerless as a result. The good news is that you have the power to create your own thriving destiny. You have the power within you to ask, and the equal ability within to receive.

THE SECRET OF INTENTION

The *Secret of Intention* is to focus on a specific quality you would like to feel rather than an exact outcome and then let it go. For example, if you want a new job you *enjoy*, imagine yourself feeling prosperous and happy at work rather than rigidly holding onto a specific job or company. This allows for the highest possibility to come in given the feeling tone you are focusing on.

Once you set your intention, *Relax* your grip - this is key! Make space. Set your intention free just like you do when dropping a love letter in a mailbox and trusting the mailman to deliver. Simply, set your intention, see it clearly happening in your mind's eye with appreciation as if it is already done, and then let it go, trusting that the same intelligence that works to heal knee scrapes, bruises, and broken bones, offers equal loyalty and responsiveness to your clear, genuine, heart-felt asking. Although the response doesn't always look exactly as you envisioned it, or take place within the exact time line that you requested, it always unfolds for your Highest Good one way or the other. Your job is to simply maintain a positive vibration. This is where most people go wrong. They grip and control and spin in negative attitudes when they don't get what they want the exact way they want it on their timeline. This attitude is one which only blocks the flow. If you can trust the unfolding and enjoy the process of clarifying what you want, asking for it, and imagining it as already being a reality, you are opening your energetic field to receive great things.

FATE AND DESTINY

Fate is what you were given at birth. Your eye color, your parents, and the city you were born in are all examples of fate. Destiny is what you do with that fate. Part of clarifying your intention and thriving is to get to know yourself on every level. Discover what it is that you love and enjoy.

What environments feel good to you?
What types of people do you enjoy being with?
What music and forms of art do you like?

What colors do you feel good wearing?
What foods make you feel vibrant?
What activities inspire and energize you?

It is highly beneficial to answer questions like these truthfully, especially if someone you love or are very close to has a different set of preferences than you. Often times, people get stuck in what they were given out of habit, even if they are miserable in that reality. Asking questions and beginning to explore what is genuine for **you** begins to introduce you to your unique habitat, the environment in which you personally thrive. Once you know who you are and what you want you can more readily ask for it and by doing so sculpt your destiny.

Birds flourish amidst open skies while dolphins dance under deep, sweeping seas. Yet, they can't survive in each other's habitats. One is not better than the other. They are simply different. Where do you shine? Once you discover your unique habitat, and lovingly bask in it regularly, a natural byproduct is discovering the gifts and talents that live within you. When you are relaxed and healthy, clarity around your unique purpose becomes rather automatic.

This Outer Purpose, your unique genius, is actually another form of habitat. One of the easiest ways to find your Outer Purpose is to ask yourself what is one thing you love doing so much that you are happy to do it for free? Let's say you love singing in the shower. Enjoying time each day singing, even if only in the bathroom, will then lead you to feeling empowered, replenished and alive. This is part of your innate genius, which is a form of habitat that nourishes your soul. When you regularly practice doing what you love, you fuel your spirit and raise your frequency.

In essence, you create your own destiny by weaving more and more of what you purely love into your life day by day. It is not always the easy road at first because most of us have become so accustomed to living as a false self upon someone else's pre-paved road. Yet eventually, when in each and every moment you follow the path that is most compelling to your heart, and prioritize your own self-care (especially when logic convinces you otherwise), you shed that which no longer serves you and find yourself living a fulfilling, authentic life that you love.

TRUSTING THE JOY OF YOUR INNER ESSENCE

As Joseph Campbell said "Follow your bliss and the Universe will open doors for you where there were only walls." Your passion, genuine desire, and heartfelt dreams are whispers from your core design, which drive you forward towards your **Unique Destiny** and Outer Purpose. Anything is possible when you prioritize what you love. As a child, you already knew what this was because it is what you couldn't help but enjoy doing. It may have been singing, dancing, painting, role-playing as a business person or doctor, baking, fixing things, or perhaps as simple as saving snails and climbing trees. Our natural gifts and proclivity towards certain daydreams and activities are clues for each of us to pay attention to in finding our bliss.

Imagine a glorious oak tree. Before it even materializes, the oak tree drives the intelligence within the acorn to awaken it from a safe, dormant state into the adventure of growth, expression, and thriving expansion. The full-potential Oak provokes the first sprout to courageously break through the safe (but limited) seed, surpassing any weeds, rubble, or obstructions as it intuitively reaches straight towards the sun.

As individuals, we too are encoded with a unique design that inspires us toward our own destiny, yet unlike an acorn, we have both conscious choice and powerful awareness. We have the ability to set our intentions to create the proper inner conditions that are necessary for us to thrive. We have the ability to clear the weeds of negative thinking and surrender to the passion, joy, and talents that genuinely inspire and uplift us.

Isn't this exciting?! You are alive and have been given the power to make your life a living, inspiring masterpiece, like any wonderful book, heroic film, or amazing work of art. This power is yours to use by entering your intention into your navigation system so that rather than ending up somewhere you'd rather not be... AGAIN... you can consciously lead your own life upon terrain that you truly love. In the same way that every plant and animal has a function, you too have a unique function known as your purpose.

Once you awaken to your unique habitat and gifts without comparing yourself to others, then you are able to flourish and contribute more to the whole, peacefully and freely. It actually becomes easy to ask for what you need clearly and lovingly when you know who you are so deeply and intimately. Tending to yourself becomes as natural as watering and tending to a garden. You simply see what is needed and you respond to fulfill it's needs.

One of the easiest ways to get to know yourself is by connecting with your **Inner Essence** by looking back on what you loved as a child and asking the **In-**

ner Child within you, which is still very much alive in you now, what he/she wants from your life today. Whenever I feel overwhelmed, depleted, or tense, it's a clear indicator that I have not been attuned to my *Inner Essence*, which is precisely when I turn to my *Inner Child* and listen to what she needs.

In the process of writing this book and spending many extra hours on my computer, my *Inner Child* became deflated. This became obvious because my joy started dwindling. When I checked in with her, she was so happy to feel my *Presence* and attention. Through the years, this inner relationship has created a great deal of self-trust and accountability. When I asked her what she needed, she knew immediately: a weekly swim in the ocean. At first, it seemed impossible to find the time. Yet, as we know the word "impossible" itself says I'm Possible! So, of course, I found a way to "create" the time and when I did, the benefits were exponential.

Taking these 2-3 hours a week while writing this book not only kept me balanced and playful, it also inspired me to get into wonderful physical shape. Somehow, being under the sun and in a bikini inspired me to get away from social media for the most part and use the freed up time to start running again and practicing yoga. These lifestyle changes transformed my body, my sense of empowerment, and my level of joy in a radical manner. Although tuning into the *Inner Child* may seem a bit airy fairy or maybe even a nuisance to some, the benefits of heeding the guidance of your *Inner Essence* run incredibly deep.

Stillness Heals and Illuminates Natural Energy

I invite you to completely drop everything that you've just read, trusting that whatever is in your highest good is already integrated and available when you need it. Relax your jaw, loosen your belly, soften your hips and shoulders, and simply breathe consciously into your body, bringing full awareness and energy back to yourself. For the next couple of minutes, feel free to close your eyes and empower the 3 B's: Breath, Body Awareness, Brow Center. Remember, your body benefits greatly and relaxes when you breathe into it and are Present with it. Explore for yourself and when you feel complete, open your eyes and enjoy the following practice.

Your Gem Power Declaration

I AM intentionally co-creating my reality in accordance with my heart's pure, joyful, genuine desire.

Diamond Self Activation

Putting it into Practice...

1. CREATE A VISION BOARD AND HANG IT IN YOUR SPACE OF LOVE:
Harvest images and quotes that inspire you from old magazines or print them from the Internet. Create a collage on a poster board, canvas, or a simple sheet of paper. Personally, my vision board is a collection of inspiring images tacked to a rustic piece of wood and hung near my writing desk.

The key is to collect and arrange high-vibrational images that inspire your heart and feel good to look at. This board is a visual intention of what you would like your life to look like in an ideal world. Once you finish it, hang it up in your **Space of Love** or somewhere you will see it regularly.

2. PRACTICE ASKING FOR WHAT YOU NEED:
Remember, nearly everything that you want is outside of your comfort zone. Push your edges by communicating what you need more openly with loved ones, the people you interact with on a daily basis, and in prayer. The key here is to ask lovingly, clearly, and free of attachment to the outcome. Your asking in itself is a form of empowerment. If the person you ask is not able to give you what you want, this is a great opportunity to let go of attachment and discover the best way for you to respond from this new point of awareness.

3. SET YOUR MORNING INTENTION, BEDTIME INTENTION, SCENE INTENTION:
Start with one of these forms of intention (i.e. morning intention) and become aware of the difference it makes in your day. From there, add another form of intention (i.e. scene intentions) and discover what practices work best for you.

4. WEEKLY DIAMOND DATE:
Do something you LOVE and vibrate with your vision.
Right now, in this **Present Moment**, ask yourself **why** you want what you

want. What quality is driving your want? In other words, once you have the outcome of your desire, what will you feel? Then, find a way to *feel* that now. For example, when I wanted more money, I realized what I really wanted was freedom to enjoy my life. So, I started to enjoy my life immediately by relaxing in nature where I was free of technology and massaging my feet with coconut oil. *Why* do you want what you want? What quality are you desiring to embody more of in your life? What activity supports this now? Enjoy your weekly *Diamond Date!*

5. QUALITY - NORTH STAR INTENTION:

Once you clarify the quality you are wanting to embody more of in your life, create a **North Star** intention around the quality and post it where you can see it daily (the refrigerator or bathroom mirror are great spots for your post). For example, if you would like to embody more Authenticity in your life, your **North Star** Intention may be, *"My intention is to embody Authenticity in my life with ease, love, and freedom."*

6. DIAMOND DREAM SHEETS:

Choose one area of your life you would like to upgrade and map your vision of how you would like it to look in an ideal world by using the following steps.

1. Create your own Diamond Dream Sheet similar to the illustration below. At the top of the page, choose the area of your life that you would like to upgrade and title your dream scene accordingly.
   i.e. *Joyful Career, Financial Prosperity, Radiant Health, etc.*

2. Each line is for a new sentence. Feel free to add more lines if you feel inspired to.
3. Use colored pens or add images if you feel inspired to. Get creative with the sheets. ***The more heart you put into them, the easier and more expediently you attract your vision into manifestation. If you feel good making them, you are on the right track.***
4. Make sure each sentence is at least 50% believable to you. For example, if you are currently making $50,000 a year, but want more financial abundance, start with writing about how you are currently making (a maximum of) $100,000 since in this example, $100,000 would be 50% believable already.
5. Make sure to always add a blanket statement at the bottom of the page that reads: *"This or something better for the Highest Good of All Concerned with Ease and Grace."* This leaves room for an even greater possibility than you can imagine right now to come in for you with ease.

HAVE FUN WITH THIS.
PUT ON MUSIC, LIGHT A CANDLE, BREATHE DEEPLY,
     AND ENJOY BEING A CONSCIOUS CO-CREATOR OF YOUR DESTINY...
ALL FOR THE HIGHEST GOOD HERE AND NOW!

DIAMOND SELF ACTIVATION (JOURNAL QUESTIONS)

* How could you listen more deeply to your Higher Self and intuition?

* What stops you from asking for help from a higher power?

* Is it easy or difficult for you to ask for what you need from those around you?

* What is one thing you could ask for and from whom within the next 24 hours? This is your chance to build your "ask for help clearly and free of attachment" muscles.

> "There is a crack, a crack in everything.
> That´s how the light geths in."
> Leonard Cohen

Week Three: Awareness
Seeing Triggers as Treasures

For the first 30+ years of my life, I was endlessly swallowed up and spit out by the tides of my own emotions; recklessly tossed around by anger, and helplessly sucked in through fear, while suddenly and surprisingly being propelled to the highest crests of joy, only to so easily crash back down into grief. This cycle continued, in all of it's many and varied combinations, as I did my best to cling to the highs, while I desperately tried to avoid the lows. My futile attempts at such only intensified this frustrating tug.

I eventually found a surfboard, and when that happened I realized that I could ride the waves of emotion rather than getting slammed by them. This "surf board" is not something that I bought at a sports shop. No! In fact, this "surf board" happens to be a simple foundational instrument that one finds in the power of ***Awareness**.* The most wonderful news is that this power is available to you now within your consciousness.

As I briefly covered earlier, **Awareness** is one of the five attributes of the **Diamond Self**. **Awareness** is a state of mind that allows us to see life as it is, clearly and without judgment. If Presence is a state of being, **Awareness** is a spacious state of mind that allows you to embrace life openly and fully without it becoming part of your identity.

Imagine the difference between being slammed by a wave in the ocean and using it to skillfully, effortlessly, and joyfully glide back to the dependable shore. Being on top of the wave, rather than beneath it, not only shifts the experience, but also gives one a very different perspective. It's from this surfboard that you can finally see, with amazing clarity, that you are not the wave of anger. Now you are simply the witness who is watching the wave as it swells, then crests, then recedes.

When you believe that you are your thoughts, your emotions, or even your body, suffering is inevitable given the never-ending up and down reality of duality (not to mention the impermanence). When you activate the gem of **Awareness** you migrate to the **Diamond Self**. It's from this place within that you begin to live life from the unbreakable and eternal dimensions of **Love** and **Oneness**.

The easiest way to empower **Awareness** is to slip into the **I AM** witness at the heart of the **Diamond Self**. Simply notice what you are thinking right now, including the sensations in your body and how you are feeling emotionally, without giving it a "meaning" or a "story." It's like scanning a car for any damage before you rent it. You simply walk around the car and notice where there are dings and scratches. You may even notice certain features of the car. There is no story or drama, just a tracking of what is present.

Anything you can see, hear, taste, smell, and touch is part of the **Present Moment**. Remember that the **Diamond Self** is **aware** of what is tangible in the Now with boundless Presence, including any **Awareness** of thoughts about the past and future. Rather than believing your thoughts, you become silently alert and awake to each thought as it arises, which frees you from being lost beneath a wave of emotional thoughts, to seeing the lay of the emotional landscape from greater altitude.

A beautiful example of someone who leads from a state of pure **Awareness** is Amma, the hugging saint from India, who has hugged many millions of people. I have personally received hugs from Amma on multiple occasions and from this experience, one thing that I realized is that she embraces everyone equally. A stressed father, a homeless woman, and an innocent child will all receive the same compassionate, loving embrace. She even passes out chocolate kisses and a flower. Amma does not judge what she sees, but simply includes all beings within her sphere of **Awareness** and spaciousness.

Suffering is the result of attempting to escape or change what is. Freedom is being aware of life in the moment and simply feeling what you feel without judging it or getting lost in it.

THE POWER OF AWARENESS

I remember hiking up a mountainous trail years ago that I had probably hiked at least one hundred times before. It was my favorite park, yet it had become so familiar to me that I couldn't help but anticipate each curve well before I was there. I knew where the bunnies were going to be, which tree was just around each bend, as well as the patch of fine sand that comforted my step at the base of the valley.

On this especially gorgeous morning I just happened to be the only person on the trail. For whatever reason, at some particular point along the trail I spontaneously stopped in my tracks as I allowed my playful, childlike *Inner Essence* to get the best of me.

I imagined that I had just been dropped on Earth for the first time in this very body, on that very stretch of land... alone and not knowing anything, including where I was, or even my name. I let my mind go blank... EMPTY! I looked down at my feet against the beige packed dirt, becoming utterly present and focused on the textures of my shoes and the sparkling particles of minerals within the dirt.

The surge of awe that rose through me sent me into a spin, literally, as I raised my gaze to take in all that surrounded me. I twirled and hopped and sprung. I played with every leaf. I looked at my hands and breathed the air. In response to the beautiful golden light of the vast blue sky set against the green, tree laden mountains, I felt an immense wellspring of emotion surge within me. For the first time in my life I was seeing the world around me and I felt so magnificently alive. It was as if I was walking upon a sparkling gem as every step reflected the miraculous. I knew nothing and in knowing nothing I felt so much joy and possibility. My instincts were to touch the dusty sand, smell the wild flowers, and outstretch my arms at the sight of a bird.

When my mind emptied, my body awakened. The very hike that I knew like the back of my hand had at once become a mystery that I was eager to explore. Without an ounce of self-consciousness, I was free to see life through the eyes of the sheer *Awareness* of what is. WOW!

Feeling that memory all over again as I am writing this, a bird suddenly flew to my window. Without a reason, she seemed to look straight at me as she fluttered her wings to remain at eye level. The only thing separating us was a simple pane of glass. In the same way, the window pane of one's incessant thinking and self-consciousness can separate one from experiencing life as the boundless miracle that it is.

Just like the glass, we become so accustomed to thoughts and beliefs standing between our hearts and truth that we lose our connection with what is fresh and alive. As children, we eventually learned to wall ourselves behind a pane of right and wrong, thus "thinking our way" out of authenticity. In doing so we pressed our feelings down in our innocent attempts to be loved by people within environments that were too small for our wild hearts. We had to find a way to fit in, to tame our glorious roars in order to be accepted by those we loved and depended on. This marked the beginning of getting lost in self-consciousness and distancing ourselves from our own unique, authentic essence.

SELF-AWARENESS VERSUS SELF-CONSCIOUSNESS

There is a radical difference between *Self-Awareness* and self-consciousness. Being *Self-Aware* involves seeing yourself as you are, feeling what is present within, both light and dark, without getting lost in a story about it. As the great spiritual teacher Krishnamurti once said, "The highest form of human intelligence is to observe yourself without judgment." *Self-Awareness* is powerful. It provides you with a "distance" from what you are feeling and thinking so you can observe the situation, and what you are feeling, rather than being tossed around by it. *Self-Awareness* is greatly freeing, bringing a gentle loving quality to yourself rather than frantically squirming around for external approval.

On the other hand, self-consciousness is dominated by worrying about how others perceive you, getting lost in other people's opinions, and allowing others to create your personal identity. For example, that morning on my hike I noticed two people walking towards me on the trail and immediately squeezed myself into "normal" as I quickly pulled my outstretched arms back to my sides and turned my gaze down to the ground.

Clearly, my self-consciousness momentarily got the best of me once I crossed paths with others on the trail. Yet rather than worrying,

"Oh Goddess! Did they see me flying around like a swooping eagle?"

"Did they hear me coo and caw with the ravens overhead? Do they think I am a straight up looney bird?"

I drew my attention within instead as I became aware of the shift in my body language and embraced the part of me that wanted to hide, breathing deeply and lovingly into the subtle constriction.

Moments later my self-consciousness had dissolved into **Self-Awareness** as I noticed how quickly I got pulled out of my wildly-free, authentic self and how my body language and energy had so rapidly collapsed.

I didn't judge myself or them for ruining a perfect moment. I simply watched the unfolding as if watching myself and the two people like characters in a movie. It was actually interesting and entertaining to discover. When you can witness yourself without judgment in the same way you watch a movie, you know that you've entered the transformational realm of **Self-Awareness**. This is also evidence that you are living your Inner Purpose.

As you embody the **Diamond Self**, focusing on fitting in falls away bit by bit as **Self-Awareness** replaces self-consciousness. Every moment becomes an opportunity to free your joy and wildness from the grips of a painfully groomed world. When the power of **Awareness** sets in, we experience relaxed stability and what it is to be authentically honest and alive. In the same way that a child can be totally entertained by a patch of grass and a few sticks, when the attribute of **Awareness** is strengthened, our senses awaken, sovereignty grows, and life becomes fun and enchanting once again.

THE SOUL'S HUNGER

Have you ever noticed that what drives all of your actions in your day-to-day life is a deep hunger to find lasting joy, peace, or freedom? If you are anything like me, and the journey that I found myself traversing for countless years, no matter what you do, try to do, or even achieve, nothing seems to satiate that deep, mysterious hunger within, at least not for long.

In moments of discomfort when you brush up against the strange sense of emptiness inside, you may find yourself going shopping to buy a new pair of shoes, treating yourself to a delicious meal, or directing all of your attention to either finding a new job or a different relationship. Yet, once you buy the shoes, eat the decadent dessert, land the new job, or fall in love, at some point that pleasure will slowly evaporate. When this happens, what you are left with is the same sense of emptiness that prompted you to begin this search for happiness outside yourself in the first place.

If this is you, then **congratulations!** Nothing has worked for very long because your hunger runs far deeper, calling from a place inside that settles for nothing less than total freedom and fulfillment. Clearly you are ready to hear and respond to this calling, otherwise it wouldn't be coming up and you certainly wouldn't be reading this book. Life only gives us what we are prepared to handle in any given moment, however temporarily uncomfortable it may be.

When we feel lost, lonely, or empty, it is simply a cue that we are running away from ourselves and as long as we run or hide, we will never be free. As long as we are not free, we will never know true love.

We all have facets of ourselves that have long been hidden and sometimes even buried. The lack of access to these parts of yourself creates discomfort and a sense that something is missing. The good news is that when, due to being triggered by either a person or event, your life seems to be falling apart, this is merely a sign that your soul is giving you a nudge. This is happening in an attempt to prompt you to stop reaching for the scraps of pleasure and validation that others toss your way, to sitting at the head of the table enjoying the gourmet meal of Radical Self-Love that never runs out. The soul hungers for you to be whole and **Present** through any circumstance and it is in the midst of this cracked-open discomfort that the great treasure of true power can open into your life.

TRIGGERS AS TREASURES

Anything that pulls you out of Presence and into negative thinking, criticism, or a feeling of upset, is a trigger. These emotions have appeared to let you know that there's hurt somewhere inside of you that's calling for your tending. Again, as discussed in chapter two, "rubble"(Repressed Unconscious Beliefs and Blocks of Locked Emotion) is what stands in the way of being fully present and self-expressed in each moment. "Rubble" is the shield over the **Diamond Self** in the same way that the excess marble around Michelangelo's "David" kept the angel from being fully revealed in our world.

Triggers are actually our friends, for they show us where we are weighed down by the rubble that limits our light and power. Triggers come in various forms and levels of severity that range from having a health scare, to someone dying in the family, or having a tiff with a good friend, or even getting a divorce. It's important for you to realize that triggers and interruptions do not come into your life to destroy you. Instead, when they are approached from a place of **Awareness**, they actually stimulate growth as they show you where there is room for more self-care and greater self-acceptance.

THE TROUBLE WITH AVOIDING THE "RUBBLE"

One of the downfalls I often see in people on the spiritual path is that they are so used to doing and striving to become better that they avoid the ***Present Moment*** without even realizing it. The most common habit I see during private sessions is as soon as negative emotion comes up and I guide the client to breathe into it and be fully present with the feeling with ***Awareness*** and curiosity, something opens. Perhaps this is simply a few tears being shed. Yet whatever opens, rather than staying with it, they almost immediately go into their head and begin to talk their way around the discomfort.

Thinking and talking are the ways that we avoid feeling. The problem with this pattern is that we never allow ourselves to accept the feeling and integrate this facet of ourselves that was left behind long ago. As we continue to abandon various parts of ourselves, the feeling of emptiness lingers, which perpetuates the feelings of being lost and alone. Building a new "muscle" of feeling into the moment, versus thinking about the past and future, is how we open the door to access the treasure. The trigger is simply the doorbell ringing, prompting you to open the door and welcome the long lost treasure that is available here and now.

I once worked with a client in his mid-sixties who experienced painfully gripping gastritis, which had him in complete agony much of his days. In fact, the pain had become so unbearable that he was contemplating suicide. In his quest to find healing, he'd tried everything from a myriad of "proper diets" to various healers and specific treatments. However, in one session with me, we found the root of this punishing pain, which happened to be a screeching cry from his inner child who was tired of hiding and fearing the world.

Being that there is always an unmet need at the center of our pain, it was just a matter of time to find his own unmet need. For this man, his inner child simply declared that he pay attention to him and invite him in for the long haul with gentleness, priority, and patience. This starved inner child knew that he needed to receive the tenderness that he'd never received from his parents. He'd finally identified an essential need that required him to come to peace with life, experience his own wellbeing, and blossom.

In facing the rubble, a new lease on life was granted to a man who was on the verge of taking his life. Once he stopped running from the pain and went right into the center of it with openness and loyalty, a miracle presented itself. Within the mess there is always a message... a map of sorts to the miracle. All that is required of someone to experience this is a willingness to turn to it and listen.

Most people chase their tails as they attempt to rearrange their life circumstances in a gallant effort to fix things "out there." Yet what they fail to realize is that the real attention needed is to what is happening within. Rather than developing a powerful inner Presence, they spin out their wheels as they fight with life's details by over-thinking each and every one of them. Humanity is lost on the surface in a never-ending reaction to "what is." This exhausting road to nowhere finally ends once we stop in our tracks, allow ourselves to let go of the dizzying drama, and become still and Present with what we are feeling as we deepen in friendship with ourselves.

The doorway into this transformation has nothing to do with thinking, judging, or hiding, and everything to do with feeling, loving, and breathing into our aching hearts... an ongoing experience that's so much simpler than we "think."

For example, imagine asking someone for directions. As soon as you ask them, they know exactly where to direct you, pointing their finger to indicate the direction of your destination.

Rather than saying *"thank you"* and heading off in the direction of their pointing, you first grab their pointer finger and try to find your way by examining their pointer finger, first bending it, then pulling it, and finally twisting it to no avail. While this analogy probably made little if any sense, neither does the way in which most of us react to life's challenges. Similarly to someone's index finger communicating that you need to "go that way" to reach your destination, triggers are simply guiding you to turn within rather than focusing on the drama out there. Triggers are always a signal that there is work to be done inside of yourself.

When we get stuck on the trigger, we remain lost. When we think incessantly about somebody who wronged us rather that putting all of that energy into being with our own feelings, listening deeply within, and breathing into the body, we completely miss the intended path. In reality, the trigger is nothing more than a doorbell ringing to reveal an unresolved, disowned part of the self that is inviting integration (Wholeness). The limited ego leads us to fearfully judge, run from, and mask pain, which is like putting a Band-aid over a gaping war wound. The **Diamond Self** opens, observes, and embraces the pain, bringing love and tenderness that allows lasting healing to take place.

More often than not your greatest challenge today is the result of something that you chose to believe as early as the age of three, before rational thinking had even developed. The truth is, today's triggers are living maps that direct you to treasure chests that had long ago fallen overboard and were lost when life itself became too much to handle and impossible to process.

Today these treasures remain beneath what mystics have described as a "sea of grief." They simply lie in wait at the bottom, ready for you to dive deep into reclaiming what is wonderfully yours. When you realize that without these very triggers there would be no way of discovering what has been holding you back from clearly and confidently moving forward, facing these challenges becomes a grand opportunity for you to chisel away at what's blocked your "angel."

Once you see, through loving eyes, the obstacle you were once unaware of, a door opens to reveal a pathway that leads you to YOU... a path that returns you to love. Most of us never realize there is a constructive way to deal with discomfort, nor do we realize that it usually has nothing to do with this moment and everything to do with locked emotion from the past that was never given the opportunity to express itself.

As human beings, when faced with a challenging trigger, the fight or flight reaction ignites within us, which is sheer animal instinct. If we are to awaken beyond the level of consciousness of a monkey or donkey, we will need to open up to a higher way of responding to life and, believe it or not, your very triggers are gateways into this elevated level of consciousness.

THE SOUL'S CURRICULUM

Earth is not a place, it is really a process or school that stimulates learning, growth, and ideally, freedom. Whatever you are going through right now is your soul's curriculum. Most people never access the ***Diamond Self*** because they are constantly running from their triggers. By doing this they drop out of the very life classes that are designed to evolve them out of their limitations and into wholeness, which is what their soul hungers for the most.

Personally, one of my soft spots or common triggers is the thought of my beloved partner, Jason, lying to me or somehow betraying me. This is my soul's curriculum. Many times, this weakening thought has made me want to engage my old pattern by running for the hills, and thus avoiding the possibility of him either disappointing or hurting me. The truth is, though, that there is a treasure to be found in this triggering fear... running would never grant me the key to my camouflaged fortune. The only way to get **through** this is by going through it by being present with "what is," and doing so indicates a radical shift in consciousness. This marks the beginning of something miraculous as we're steered away from mediocrity and into our magnificence!

Imagine if Michelangelo tried to avoid the excess marble. He never would have been able to reveal "The David." When triggered by bad news, a person who pisses you off, a challenging situation, or really anything "out there" that disturbs your peace, counter to popular belief, the opportunity is to drop the obsession with trying to fix or change what "needs to be done" "out there," and instead lovingly go towards the feeling of discomfort within you. Loving yourself deeply is how you master the inevitable lessons of life. True peace is an inside job and pure **Awareness** and Presence with **what is** heals the pain that has blocked it.

As Thich Nhat Hanh says, *"Awareness is like the sun. When it shines on things, they are transformed."* The easiest way to begin the metamorphosis from breakdown to breakthrough is to ask yourself two questions:

1. *"What feeling is this trigger bringing up in me?"* Do you feel angry, sad, fearful, anxious, joyful? This question immediately pulls you out of dwelling on the trigger while creating healthy distance from the feeling so you can witness and heal it.
2. *"Where do I feel (this feeling) in my body?"* This question brings you into your body and since your body is truly here in the **Present Moment**, it awakens the Diamond Self.

Once you name the feeling and locate where it is in the body, simply open up to it, allow it to be, and breathe into it. I like to imagine that there's a seed at the center of the feeling, bringing my attention to the very core. Whenever I feel something uncomfortable or undesirable emotionally, I give myself permission to **consciously** dive into the center of it and feel that way all day if I need to. As soon as I do, something opens and the e(motions) begin to move.

You can also place your hands on the location where you feel the emotion or vulnerability. Since we are mammals, the warmth of our hands calms the nervous system, dropping cortisol (the stress hormone) levels in the body.

If you notice that you start to feel free in that area, yet now feel discomfort someplace else, you can move your hands to the new location and keep breathing into it. Sometimes the emotion, which is really just energy in motion, moves or migrates. This is normal and healthy and happens in most everyone.

FIGHT, FLIGHT, OR F.L.O.W.

Fight or flight is valuable when faced with life-threatening danger, such as a starved Bengal Tiger running fast and furiously towards you, but most of what we fear is far from life-threatening. Perhaps, ego-threatening, but certainly not life-threatening. The triggers we experience today are typically echoes of yesterday's hurts. They reverberate through time re-enacting through different characters again and again until we go to the root and discover what we made true about our life in the midst of those painful, long-ago moments.

In regards to living a life of love, neither fight or flight work when facing challenges. Fight is obvious: fighting, battling, blaming, hating, anger against somebody else. The reality is they may have done something cruel or awful, yet the power is in your hands to take care of yourself. Fighting another person only creates more of what you are fighting against while distracting you from tending to what you really need.

The other thing people do when facing friction is they run, or move into flight mode. They run out the door in the middle of a confrontation or quit a job after one tough day. Flight mode is simply the tendency to run or hide in the face of conflict. Oh goodness, was I an expert at that one!

There is nothing wrong with fight or flight. However you tend to deal with challenge is okay. Yet with this I am simply offering you another possibility, which I call:

F.L.O.W. - or - **F**ueling **L**ove **O**ver **W**ar. (Yes, another acronym... surprise!)

The question is do you choose to fight against the source of pain in your life or run away from it (which is simply a disguised form of battle)? With either choice, you never really heal the issue. However when you choose to feel what is genuinely present in you, and therefore **F.L.O.W.** in your life, you liberate your inner source of radiant health? How do we F.L.O.W. when we feel anger, resentment, blame or shame, pain, and self-pity?

FLOW utilizes the painful trigger to wake up to higher consciousness and lovingly move towards yourself rather than away. For the most part, it has nothing to do with the other person who's presented you with this challenge, aside from them having made you *aware* of your soul's curriculum. Therefore, FLOW mode can be chosen without needing anyone else's actions to change. Rather than the learned habit of suppression through blame (i.e. fight mode) or denial (i.e. flight mode), you have the power to discharge the emotion and come into a truce with what you are feeling inside by opening up to another attribute of the *Diamond Self*... **Authenticity**.

'FESS UP AND RISE UP

The reason most of us are lost in the animal instinct of fight or flight comes down to habit. Have you ever noticed yourself fighting with your lover or snapping at your child even though you feel terrible about it while in the midst of it? Do you ever feel like you can't control your reactions, as if they are happening even though you'd prefer to respond calmly and lovingly?

Most of our habits today are learned behaviors that don't even belong to us, but are simply conditioned reactions that were modeled to us, especially by our parents and guardians. These conditionings created neural pathways in the brain that make us gravitate to each particular reaction every time we are faced with the same stimuli.

Let's say you take something personally and feel hurt by a comment that was made by your husband or wife. The conditioned habit may be to lash out (fight) or storm out of the room (flee). Both of these repress what you are really feeling and never resolve anything. Meanwhile, the neural pathway in the brain deepens, becoming a stronger groove every time you repeat that specific reaction.

Neural pathways and habits cannot be destroyed. They can only be overridden by new habits. Since suppression or refraining from asking for what you deeply need tends to be at the root of disempowerment (via fight or flight), when you empower the new habit of being present with what you feel, clarifying your needs, and authentically expressing yourself (privately or with your loved ones), you can start to rise up out of the old, limiting grooves. You have this power!

Empowering the attribute of **Authenticity** through what I call, 'fessing up and rising up,' by getting real with what you feel, is one powerful way of freeing yourself from the rubble to fuel a new pattern of love. One of the easiest ways to do this is to find a sentence that expresses the most honest, vulnerable reality concerning your challenge and just let it be. Notice how it feels to allow this messy truth to exist without a knee-jerk attempt to get rid of it.

For example, years ago I worked with a client who desperately wanted to lose twenty pounds and had already tried every diet that existed. Nothing worked. She had been chasing her tail for decades only to find that the weight remained. In one of our sessions, I asked her what the hardest truth she could 'fess up to was. She started on about how much she hated the extra weight on her body. With a little prompting to go deeper, she began 'fessing up to a few more things before pausing and finally saying, *"I feel like a fat worthless crumb."*

I will always remember how specific her words were and how freeing it was for her to say it out loud. She had discovered a core belief that she was worthless, as well as a facet of herself that she desperately wanted to release. Something about her saying it aloud helped her to own the fact that this was one of many parts of who she is. By voicing it's very core essence she was surprisingly brought to freeing laughter as she recognized this was simply one sliver of her reality, and just as valuable as the rest of her to exist. From there, her homework was to exaggerate the feeling of being a *"worthless crumb"* and to walk around in it's shoes all week, as if playing a character in a movie. Ironically, she made peace with this side of herself, discovered it's treasure of radical self-acceptance, and her body image skyrocketed as a result.

To come into **FLOW** requires 'fessing up to what we can't accept about ourselves and learning to ride the waves of our own emotions rather than condemning, avoiding, or trying to change them. The reality is that when we get lost in thinking, we suffer. When we return *Home* to being, we prosper. In 'fessing up, we give a voice to what we were running from, which instantaneously returns us to being.

Giving yourself permission to speak the unspeakable, for example, in the sacred space of your own journal or Space of Love, is one way to empower the greatest love affair of all, the one in which you become the lover of YOU, making choices in each moment that support you in claiming the *Treasure* within!

Stillness Heals and Illuminates Natural Energy

    I invite you to completely drop everything you have just read, trusting that whatever is in your highest good has already been integrated and is available when you need it. Relax your jaw, loosen your belly, soften your hips and shoulders, and simply breathe consciously into your body, bringing full **awareness** and energy back to yourself. For the next couple of minutes, feel free to close your eyes and empower the 3 B's: Breath, Body **Awareness**, Brow Center. Remember, your body benefits greatly and relaxes when you consciously breathe into it and are Present with it. Explore for yourself and when you feel complete, open your eyes and enjoy the following practice.

Your Gem Power Declaration

I AM using outer challenges to liberate the love within me as I radically accept myself.

Diamond Self Activation
Putting it into Practice...

1. BOUNDARY SETTING:

Expanding into *Self-Awareness* requires setting healthy boundaries so that you can hear your own heart outside of other people's input, opinions, and expectations. Temporarily (or permanently) removing the stimuli of "should's" opens up the space for you to discover your truth, genuine needs, and to finally get to know yourself.

If you have children, obviously there are valid expectations of you as a mother or father, requiring that you tend to, care for, and protect them. Yet, if you choose, you can still find a 30-minute window each day to devote entirely to your own growth in *Self-Awareness* and Self-Care. If you want to have a practice, but are convinced you don't have the time for it, then I suggest one hour instead of 30 minutes, as this is a sure sign that you will especially benefit from prioritizing yourself.

To start, make a list of all of your responsibilities and the people you tend to interact with on a regular basis. Circle the names of people who drain your energy. It's likely that you don't have clear, healthy boundaries with the people who drain you, otherwise you would feel great in their presence. You may let those people know that you are not available for the next month, six weeks, or whatever time period resonates for you as you prioritize your spiritual path and your *Diamond* journey.

It is always empowering to communicate that your lack of availability is not personal, you are simply choosing to care for your-

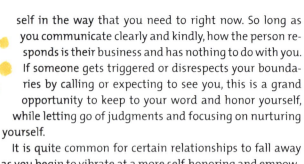

self in the way that you need to right now. So long as you communicate clearly and kindly, how the person responds is their business and has nothing to do with you. If someone gets triggered or disrespects your boundaries by calling or expecting to see you, this is a grand opportunity to keep to your word and honor yourself, while letting go of judgments and focusing on nurturing yourself.

It is quite common for certain relationships to fall away as you begin to vibrate at a more self-honoring and empowered frequency. You may find that you simply do not resonate with people you once enjoyed spending time with. If this is the case, you may find comfort knowing that this is healthy. Some friendships and relationships are temporary, while others last a lifetime. One is not better than the other. Each connection is valuable and offers unique lessons along the way.

2. FLOW JOURNAL: 'FESS UP AND RISE UP:

As you deepen into the *Present Moment*, a natural byproduct is that you will begin to see and feel what has been running you; whether love or fear... being or thinking. Awakening the treasure within requires looking at everything, especially your motives behind what you say and do, your reactions to those ever-present triggers, as well as what strengthens and weakens you in your life.

Why do you want what you want? How do you respond to triggers? Do you fight? Do you flee? Or do you fight, then flee? As the *Present Moment* becomes your priority, you will naturally get to know yourself on a deeper, more intimate level. As you begin to know yourself, your life will begin to radically transform.

One of the ways to support this magnificent shift to leading your life with love is by using a Flow Journal. Ideally, you carry this journal with you and track every time you get triggered. What triggered you? How did you react? What is the most honest thing you can say about how this trigger made you feel? What beliefs are coming up as a result of the trigger? As you get it all down on paper, you are empowering your highest form of intelligence, *Self-Awareness*, and migrating away from self-criticism, judgment, and fear.

The key to the **FLOW** Journal is for you to figuratively "unpack every box." Take an honest, thorough look at yourself! You may notice that you bragged about some achievement at a dinner party to gain approval, or rather than being present with your lover, you were caught in your head thinking about how your body looked and felt to him or her. You may also notice that you are constantly disappointed by your finances.

The key with this journal is to keep it with you throughout the day and track what pulls you out of Presence, and thus out of your **Diamond Self**. Notice what saddens, angers, or terrifies you. Be honest with what you are unwilling to accept. You will be amazed at what you discover. So long as you don't judge yourself for what you find, but simply use it as material for your inner work in the following chapters, you are radically empowering the treasure within you as you begin to harness the power of **Awareness**.

3. TRIGGERS AS TREASURES (SHINE TIME WITH EMOTIONS):

Begin by clarifying one example of someone or something that recently triggered you the most. First, identify the trigger in one sentence. i.e. *"I feel triggered because ..."* If you feel triggered, but don't know why you feel triggered, that is okay. Simply go on to the next step.

Secondly, clarify what emotion you are feeling and where you feel it in your body. i.e. *"I feel grief/heaviness in my heart and belly."*

Recognize that this is only the "rubble" (Repressed Unconscious Beliefs and Blocks of Locked Emotion), and not you! Are you willing to let the emotion be there and allow it to move however it needs to move? Now, bring the feeling into your SHINE Time practice. Simply breathe into your body and rather than focusing on your brow center, inwardly bring your soft attention to the feeling in your body.

The key is: **Don't let the feeling become thinking.** Simply, be with the feeling in your body as if you are holding an upset baby and embracing it with loyalty. As you stay with the feeling, you may notice images arise in your mind. Let them pass through like clouds blowing by in the sky.

For example, I was recently working with a client who felt grief and constriction in her heart. As she breathed into it with a sense of welcome, she spontaneously saw an image of an orange beach ball that was lodged in her chest, as if it was being stuffed down under water only to pop up again. She let go and allowed the beach ball to float in her imagery, allowing it to be there however uncomfortable it felt. After a few minutes, the heavy feeling began moving upwards, freeing up space in her heart area and leading her to confess something that she needed to share.

The key is to let go of any plan or agenda. Trying to control what is arising doesn't work. Presence heals, not a plan. Just breathe and stay **Present**. What you are feeling is part of the moment and, therefore, all that matters. Even a couple of minutes of Presence with what you feel emotionally (rather than trying to figure out why you feel this way) has tremendous, liberating power when practiced over time.

Be gentle with yourself and your process. However transformational, this practice requires repetition, time, and a clear, genuine intention to awaken into and embody the deepest level of Presence.

DIAMOND SELF ACTIVATION (JOURNAL QUESTIONS)

* What is your soul trying to teach you through your unique life story?

* What is one inspiring gem of insight you have collected from this chapter?

THE GUEST HOUSE
This being human is a guest house.
Every morning a new arrival.
A joy, a depression, a meanness,
some momentary awareness comes
as an unexpected visitor.
Welcome and entertain them all!
Even if they're a crowd of sorrows,
who violently sweep your house
empty of its furniture,
still, treat each guest honorably.
He may be clearing you out
for some new delight.
The dark thought, the shame, the malice,
meet them at the door laughing,
and invite them in.
Be grateful for whoever comes,
because each has been sent
as a guide from beyond.
~ Rumi

> *"Perhaps all the **dragons** in our lives are princesses who are only **waiting** to see us **act**, just once, with beauty and **courage**. Perhaps everything that frightens us is, in its deepest essence, something helpless that wants our love."*
> Rainer Maria Rilke

Week Four: Using Medicinal Dialogue

Like the facets of a diamond, we have various sides of our personality that collectively make up who we are. Often times, though, we have one primary facet of ourselves that we lead with, showing the world what we are most proud of, while forgetting about, or intentionally burying the rest. The truth is, in order to come into our full potential, not to mention gaining our own inner peace, each trait, or facet, needs to be accepted and integrated.

Every facet of the diamond is just as worthy of love as the rest and until we soften the fight and accept the ***whole*** of who we are, we risk losing ourselves altogether.

At your core, you are an infinite spark of consciousness that is powerful beyond measure. We are all divine beings having this human experience and when we touch this infinite, compassionate dimension inside (***Diamond Self***), it becomes second nature to accept all facets of ourselves. On a soul level, you were born to embrace every shade of your human experience until there is nothing left to hide. This is when breakdowns simply become doorways to breakthroughs.

Observing nature while I was living within the redwoods of Mendocino taught me to feel and express it all. Rather than complaining about the rain, or my own tears for that matter, I learned to strip down, open my arms wide, run wildly towards the mess, and dance **with** it. Sometimes quite literally so! Obviously, in the modern world, dropping the curtain is not the norm. Yet, it needs to be so that we can remember our worth and native origin as we begin finding our home within our hearts.

The truth is that if we lived in a world where people respected the feminine principle of life... the creative, unpredictable impulse that dances through rainbows and swaying trees to flowing rivers, tsunamis, sunrises and electrical storms, and recognize that this same perfection lives in each of us... we would finally find the freedom and happiness that we all seek. We would stop hiding what has been shamed by our limited society and start shining no matter what.

Can you imagine the power of being totally free of comparing, editing, or criticizing yourself? It is our sacred task as an evolving humanity to free this feminine principle, to allow it, to respect it, and to serve it by trading controlling, critical thoughts for authentic songs and joyful celebration. At the very least we can allow this within our own sacred Spaces of Love where we can privately discover who we authentically are and remember our Wholeness.

YOU ARE BEYOND COMPARISON!

Burying our feelings with incessant over-thinking in an attempt to fit into what is unnatural has become an epidemic, leading to an outrageous level of drug addiction (legal and illegal) and illness, including obesity. A roar is crying from within each of us to feel what we feel... *freely* and *lovingly*. Although we have found a way to turn the volume of the soul-voice down to a muted hum, we cannot escape the Love that awaits to be freed from within us. No matter how many layers of weight we put on, how many sexual obsessions we toy with, or how many chemicals, credit cards, or distracting dramas we abuse, stuffing away the pain never actually resolves it. Just as happened with me, at some point in time these stuffed feelings rise up to say,

"please look at me... and love me, too."

Are you ready? In this chapter, we are exploring the practice of **Medicinal Dialogue**, which puts the power back in your hands to discover your own needs, truth, and authentic voice. It is the heart of the **Diamond Process** and was my greatest tool during the most challenging phase of my life. With **Medicinal Dialogue**, the most important conversation of all begins to open up with the very friend who has patiently and unconditionally been with you from day one. That friend is you... and **authenticity** is the key to awakening such a bountiful friendship.

THE POWER OF AUTHENTICITY

One of the five attributes of the **Diamond Self** is **Authenticity**. What my solo journey in the redwoods taught me is that by running towards what I truly feel, rather than away from it, the great Love that I'd been seeking all along stretched her wings through my own heart to embrace it. When this happened, what I realized is that an extraordinary compassion and delicious kindness, that's not interested in perfection, lives within each of our hearts. This beautiful force honors and yields to our vulnerability.

There is strong empirical evidence demonstrating that authentic self-expression (i.e. Journaling) increases one's overall immune function and well-being. At the same time, most people fear sharing their deepest truths, thus denying the soul's impulse to heal, liberate, and rise up. The main reason most people hide their truth is to avoid others' judgments, or even worse, their own.

I created the **Diamond Process**, in part, because I was tired of the limiting opinions and advice-driven responses from people I confided in, which only stifled my truth. Regardless of their good intentions, their opinions only entangled me in even more confusion, bringing me down during an already trying time. Ideas of right-doing and wrong-doing began to sizzle my already-pained heart with a cattle brand that seemed to have permanently marked me with the word VICTIM.

I needed to process my pain, but the terrain I was traveling was too sensitive to simultaneously bear the weight of someone else's pity. I needed the dignity of my own process without being judged and labeled. I yearned to find my way back to Rumi's field, a place where I could just be an authentically expressive human without being judged or dosed with someone's agenda to fix me. Deep in my soul I knew that I just needed to find my way back to me again... the me I was before I learned to carry other people's "shoulds."

Presence is a rare commodity to find. As a human family, we yearn for compassion and connection, yet we fail to realize that we're in a world where everyone around us is as lost as we are in their own addiction to over-thinking. The good news is that you have the power to be the one you have been waiting for, embodying **Presence** in this very moment, and thus awakening the Treasure within.

Every time you are raw, honest, and tender, this great **Love** dazzles in the face of such authentic beauty, and is prepared to show off for you. If you don't believe miracles exist, I have news for you, they do! The ocean may not part, but the sea of consciousness will start to open up within your own mind every time you reveal what you truly feel, setting you free into a brand new world. They say you are only as sick as your secrets, and I say every time you embrace a facet of yourself that you thought you needed to hide, the **Diamond** that you are strengthens and shines more brightly.

When you feel stuck in fear or judgment, one of the simplest ways to create momentum and flow is to express yourself without identifying with the story. Just as the sky remains the sky while welcoming the clouds, sun, and falling snow alike, you too, have the power to activate a sense of neutrality as you genuinely express what you feel. What would it be like for you to have a temper tantrum without an ounce of self-judgment or to witness another person in deep grief without a single particle of pity or discomfort? Can you imagine the freedom?

In my early years of offering private sessions and workshops, I put forth so much unnecessary effort, only to realize that what people really wanted was the space to be seen, and accepted, and to be given a chance to genuinely express themselves. When this happens, the rest takes care of itself. My approach is certainly not like everyone else's and yet it works! Effortless, Spacious, **Compassionate Presence** sets the tone for **Authenticity** to emerge and the raw feelings to flow. As a result, one's native freedom returns home to the **Heart**. This eternal homecoming is so much simpler than we think.

Many people experience great pain as their shadows (the disowned parts of themselves) kick and scream like orphaned children who are starved for love and acceptance. For the most part, the problem is that the feeling of rejection is a knee-jerk response to pain, which squashes any chance for one to heal. It makes sense, though, doesn't it? If crying out loud or exposing your fear had a whole classroom laughing at you as a child, or a parent punishing you, then why in the world would we be comfortable expressing our feelings with others today? Pretending is the most natural learned response given society's set point, however painful that pretending may be.

As Anais Nin has said, *"When one is pretending, the entire body revolts."* It's not the **presence** of challenges and obstacles that hurt, it is the judgment of them and currently humanity is lost in this judgment. As a result, it's also lost in a massive amount of buried pain.

The habit of trying to hide, fix, or change "what is" stems from a judgment that something is wrong to begin with. Considering there are a lot of things that we can't change or control, this has led us into becoming a highly-depressed, obese, addicted culture. There is no other way to genuinely flourish than to courageously surrender the hiding, drop the judging, and free each facet of ourselves into a radically-accepting embrace.

We can fight it and it will hurt like hell. Yet the only sane alternative is to learn to let go and love ourselves ***totally***, through the hurt and disappointments. However grueling it may sound, what I have found is that, in practice, it is the greatest adventure and the way to leading an epic life... ***now***. As a result of this practice, we welcome endless miracles into our lives.

As the ***Diamond Self*** awakens from within, and this ***Radical Self-Acceptance*** takes place, a knowing develops that everyone is doing the best they can in each moment given their circumstances, including you. Let's face it, the lover that lies, the famous actress that steals, or the mother that rages at her child would do differently if they could, wouldn't they? At the core of all action, we are seeking love, happiness, and fulfillment, however clouded some approaches may be.

Since 90% of our actions are driven by the unconscious mind, it becomes essential to make the unconscious conscious. You can't tend to, and welcome, transformation around what you can't see. This is why it is crucial to wake up and see what stirs beneath the surface. Once you do, you consciously move forward from this new beginning.

Personally, the mega-tool I have used, and continue to use, throughout my journey is one that I call ***Medicinal Dialogue***. This is a technique that's been specifically designed to free you from limiting patterns, transform the relationship that you have with pain, and empower your full potential. I am excited to share this simple, valuable tool with you.

WHAT IS MEDICINAL DIALOGUE?

As a core practice of the ***Diamond Process***, ***Medicinal Dialogue*** is an integrative healing technique that empowers self-expression, healing, and deep peace. This process is realized by applying an Authentic, Accepting ***Presence*** (***Diamond Self***) to your own unresolved pain and upset ("rubble") by using a simple, direct dialogue technique.

For many of us there are times when we hush what we're feeling inside in order to avoid friction with others. Even though they've been hushed, these wild unexpressed emotions live on, causing havoc in our emotional and physical bodies. Through the application of *Medicinal Dialogue*, you will free your body and mind from the "rubble" of your repressed "stuff", while creating a new, empowered way of relating to what you think and feel. As a result, you will also naturally shift the way in which you communicate with others.

Through *Medicinal Dialogue*, you practice giving a voice to your feelings in honor of gaining insight into your core needs, facilitating healing at the deepest level.

HOW MEDICINAL DIALOGUE WORKS

To help you understand this a bit, allow me to paint a more detailed picture. As individuals we only see ourselves as a single entity with an individual personality. In fact, we are an individual with a personality and some different personas, or facets. Each of these facets tend to present themselves in different situations. For example, we tend to be one person at work, and yet another person in the company of our friends, while many of us show a different side of ourselves when we're around our families, and yet a different one when we're with someone we love. We also have a dimension of us that stands back and watches everything going on free of judgment... the compassionate witness (*Diamond Self*).

In this technique, the *Diamond Self* dialogues with one part, or facet, of yourself to allow the repressed emotion to be released so that it no longer has the power to create upset within you.

For example, as I'm writing this, a drill just started buzzing away next door, which has brought up some anger within me. The neighbors are building a guesthouse (illegally, I might add) yet told each of those who are neighbors that they were building a simple storage unit. They even went around to all of the neighbors, door to door, to explain that it would only take a few days, apparently as they didn't want anyone in the neighborhood to complain. However, it would appear that they lied, because every day of the week for the past four months they've been drilling, hammering, and clambering all day long.

Right now, what I really want to do is to go next door and give these people a piece of my mind, what little there is to spare. For the past four months all of this work has been polluting our living space with the noise that they create on a daily basis. Even more aggravating is that it also appears that they intentionally lied to all of us. It's not what they're doing, but the fact that it's dragging on that's become maddening.

While I prefer to respond peacefully, every time we don't allow ourselves to express out what really "wants" to be said, due to the conditioning that we've been taught, then we're trapped behind our rubble. Ironically any outburst of anger will only become stronger when it's suppressed under a mountain of "shoulds."

With that said, instead of getting mad and going next door to give them a piece of my mind, I just felt the genuine frustration arise, expressed what I really wanted to say in a few sentences, and funny enough, the noise stopped. It is amazing how often our outer world changes as it reflects our inner world. Once you make peace within (self-expression is an essential way of doing that), often times, your environment becomes friendlier as well.

Before I go any further, let me make something very clear. I am not saying that you voice your anger or other challenging emotions to the person who has "tripped your trigger." NO! This process has been specifically designed to be practiced privately in your journal, out loud in your **Space of Love**, or with a compassionate professional who is able to honor your authentic self-expression without judgment or agenda. It's simply about expressing outwardly what we have been repressing.

The world around us will continue to provide triggers in bolder and more undeniable ways. We can either use them to blossom or abuse them as excuses to contract. As the figurative drilling gets louder, our relationships will either become more tumultuous, or the body will weaken until we consciously choose to transform by responding in a new way.

Whatever one is dealing with, whether it is in the body, the mind, or in the physical world, will typically continue to get louder in order to shake us up to instigate healing, expression, and liberation of what has been repressed. It's not a punishment, but an exquisite evolution of consciousness that's happening through you in the present moment.

Pema Chodron expresses it beautifully with these words. *"Nothing goes away until it teaches you what you need to learn."*

Through the process of **Medicinal Dialogue** we begin to soften the pulsing conundrums that we call fear, anxiety, rage, disgust, disappointment, shame, blame, jealousy, and so on. We finally examine what we've avoided so that we can activate the power of consciously seeing through the eyes of the **Diamond Self**. Through this we come into a deep state of embodied **Authenticity**, **Presence**, and **Love** that naturally attracts the same love into our work, relationships, bodies, and minds. Even in the midst of a challenging day, we're able to become kind, trusting, and loving.

Most of us are unwilling to express what we really feel out of fear of abandonment, rejection, or worry that showing our true colors will create more suffering. The mind will rationalize in any way that it can to avoid expressing our "dirty feelings" and dark thoughts. However the only way to heal is to consciously shine the light on them and set free what often has been hidden from our ability to feel.

While we're taught all kinds of (mostly useless) information in school that we memorize for tests, but so easily forget, we're never taught how to manage our thoughts and feelings. It's due to this lack of *self-awareness* that everyday people have no idea how to live a vibrant, healthy, fulfilling life.

In ancient civilizations, there were countless rituals and rites of passages that prepared each individual to live in harmony with their communities, with the Earth, and themselves. Yet in modern society, rather than becoming conscious, most of the world avoids the **Diamond Self** by burying themselves in credit card debt, escaping themselves in front of their televisions, gossiping, or filling themselves with fear by taking in mainstream news. All the while they stuff themselves with fatty, processed, cancer-inducing foods, in yet another effort to avoid the feelings that they so desperately wish to run away from. The good news is that by reading this book and exposing yourself to this new paradigm, *you become the good news!*

The first step is realizing that there is a better way to live and it is available to you in this very moment.

The second step is to activate another attribute of the **Diamond Self**: *Allowance*. Allowing your *authentic* self-expression to flow dissolves resistance and increases freedom and peace.

The third step is knowing that there is a vast difference between consciously and unconsciously expressing yourself, especially your pain.

An unconscious example of expressing upset would be for me to go over to the neighbor's house and start screaming at everybody, dumping my anger all over them as I blame them for "my misery." That is unconscious because rather than taking ownership of my own feelings, I powerlessly project my inner anger on them. This is the old paradigm, which is what we are leaving as we evolve into something more empowering and loving to all.

There is a constructive way for me to address this situation. Instead I can say, *"While you said this was only going to go on for a few days, it's now been a few months. The daily noise is wearing on us. It's only fair of us to ask you for a completion date. We realize that you may have simply been optimistic when you began and now you feel sheepish to admit this. However, your communicating with us in a forthright manner will make this a lot more tolerable for everyone. To be honest, we feel a bit misled and hope that you can understand our position. Thank you for your time."*

Emotion is emotion. An outburst of rage is simply an outburst of rage. But, if we wrap a story around it, as in, *"Oh my god, they lied to us,"* that very energy of rage returns back into the body and never completes itself until perhaps, you face another trigger down the line. A conscious, yet responsible expression of rage is important to do as you avoid judging yourself for doing so. As soon as the judgment kicks in, the cycle perpetuates. Judgment is like a return ticket that sends you back to the source of the problem. On the other hand, the **Diamond Self** is the dimension of you that ensures your way Home. The difference comes down to feeling and expressing what you authentically feel freely without getting lost in a story about it.

FOLLOWING THE GUIDANCE OF YOUR DIAMOND SELF

Consciously taking your communication to the next level has great power. The core of the word "communicate" is "commune," meaning to come together, which invokes a state of **wholeness**.

I use **Medicinal Dialogue** (MD), and share it with you here, for it's ability to connect you to the inner voice of the **Diamond Self** while also making you aware of the contents of your unconscious mind. Through this practice, you will be giving a voice to what you feel triggered by while listening deeply and responding from the **Diamond Self**. As you listen and respond from a state of being (**Diamond Self**) rather than judgment (ego), you will gain access to your deeper wisdom and internal guidance system. Yet, this isn't something that happens in one dialogue, but is a lifestyle in which we love ourselves in the way that we've always wanted to be loved.

Medicinal Dialogue is ultimately an excavation tool, like a drill that's used to mine the gem that you are here to awaken and shine. With each dialogue you will discover something new as you gain powerful **Self-Awareness**. In the process you will befriend yourself and love yourself in a way that radically transforms and benefits your life.

In expressing what is true and real, free of judgment in sacred space, we lose the tendency to stuff our bodies, drain our bank accounts, and distract our minds. Once there is nothing to hide we no longer need the distraction.

I delight in those moments when I hear a client (often times, tearfully) recount the ease in which they were able to be themselves in a situation that once made them cringe. The joy that rises up in them is why I do what I do in the world. There is nothing quite like taking a clear, high-definition look at what we were running from, without the fight, and then responding with *authenticity*. When we attune to the voice of the *Diamond Self* within, peace inevitably blooms and love wins by a landslide.

HOW TO USE MEDICINAL DIALOGUE

The previous three steps of the *Diamond Process* (1. Awakening the *Diamond Self*, 2. Setting an *Intention*, and 3. Coming into *Awareness* around a trigger) prepare us for *Medicinal Dialogue*. To use *Medicinal Dialogue*, you simply give a voice to the emotion that is present within you. You may be angry at a person, upset with yourself, or perhaps you want to be healthier either physically or financially. Maybe there are certain obstacles you desire to drop or overcome. In your journal or out loud, you will have a conversation between your True Self (*Diamond Self*) and the upset facet, or persona. Coming into a conscious conversation with what you really feel allows you to step into the perspective of the *Diamond Self* and gain insight into the unconscious parts of the self that have been steering your ship that keeps sailing in the same circle.

The key to *Medicinal Dialogue* is to avoid using it to fix or change something. Although, healing often times is the result, if you dive into this practice (or any practice) with an agenda, you lose touch with the Present Moment, which is your only point of true and lasting power. I encourage you to use *Medicinal Dialogue* to deepen in *Presence*, *Self-Love,* and *Self-Acceptance*.

The magic of this process comes from letting yourself feel satisfied by humbly accepting your "flaws."

Medicinal Dialogue is most powerful when approached as a meditation, which empowers the I AM *Presence* (*Diamond Self*) to hold space for the energy you choose to dialogue with (i.e. your inner child), rather than attempting to escape. This is something that develops over time, through the course of your *Medicinal Dialogue* practice.

You create distance from the feeling that may be overwhelming you by entering into a dialogue with it, which allows you to see it from a more centered place. Over time, it becomes easier to be the energy of peace itself by witnessing the emotions that move through you rather than being squashed or overwhelmed by them. Rather than being taken down by a draining story, **Medicinal Dialogue** empowers you to rise up with **Love**, **Presence**, and **Authenticity**.

During my time of solitude in the redwoods, **Medicinal Dialogue** became my everyday practice. Although you can practice it through writing, given the privilege of space and privacy that I had, I chose to practice out loud, giving an actual voice to what I was feeling. You will have the opportunity to try M.D. through writing in the practice section at the end of this chapter, as well as vocally in Part III of this book.

In hindsight, it may seem crazy to some that I basically talked to myself for nine months straight. Ironically, the result allowed me to find my unshakable sanity. I remember joking at that time that **Medicinal Dialogue** was my M.D.; an ever-available doctor that always makes house calls! Rather than suppressing my pain with a pill, I intentionally dove into the pain with **Presence** and expressed what I felt without a speck of self-consciousness, which is the source of true healing. During that time, the thrill of being totally and utterly alive, messy, curious, raw, open, and 100% loyal to myself in the moment, like the greatest of lovers, returned to me. I never knew that I could experience such an amazing transformation.

What I have discovered through my own **Medicinal Dialogue** practice, as well as in guiding countless clients through this process, is that **being truthful with oneself in the moment heals**. The truth "sets you free." I can tell you first hand that the power of allowing my own full-spectrum **authenticity** was quite frankly my saving grace and a key to my own liberation during a time that I may not have otherwise survived.

Medicinal Dialogue taught me to be true in the moment, no matter how painful that moment felt. Uninhibited dialogue gives us an opportunity to put love and radical self-acceptance into practice. Wherever you are along your journey, I would like to remind you that every part of you is deeply lovable... every unique facet of you has wisdom and value. When you move with compassion for and allowance of what you fear or dislike about yourself, the hero of your own soul takes root, which leads your life in the direction of your truest calling. The best part is that those undesirable facets you once ran from actually hold necessary clues that support you in claiming the very qualities that you desire.

Stillness Heals and Illuminates Natural Energy

I invite you to completely drop everything you have just read, trusting that whatever is in your highest good is already integrated and available when you need it. Relax your jaw, loosen your belly, soften your hips and shoulders, and simply breathe consciously into your body, bringing full awareness and energy back to yourself. For the next couple of minutes, feel free to close your eyes and empower the 3 B's: Breath, Body Awareness, Brow Center. Remember, your body benefits greatly and relaxes when you breathe into it and are Present with it. Explore for yourself and when you feel complete, open your eyes and enjoy the following practice.

Your Gem Power Declaration

I AM expressing myself authentically and remembering that it is safe to be free, genuine, and empowered.

Diamond Self Activation
Putting it into Practice...

1. CLARIFY YOUR PRIMARY FACETS

Depending on who we are dealing with in the moment, and what our environment is, we show various sides of our personalities, like different facets on a diamond. At work, you may lead with the perfectionist facet, while you lead with a messy bum facet in your home life. Robin Williams, for example, led with the brilliant, charismatic comedian in the public eye and likely led with a very different facet in his private life.

Make a list of your primary facets by looking at all of the different places you invest your time. For example, what facet do you lead with at work, parties, home, the gym, the garden, philanthropic events, your yoga studio, with visiting family, on a call with your life coach, or in your massage therapist's office? List out all of the scenarios you find yourself in and the primary facet you lead with in each scenario.

Feel free to get creative by naming your facets. For example, the free-spirited explorer in you may have a name like Wanderlust Whisper. Tune in and have fun as you explore your primary facets. Here are some more examples:

Ms. Perfect

Busy Bee Brenda

People Pleaser Peggy

Social Sam Butterfly

Aloof Airhead

Class Clown Cray Cray

Know it all Nancy

Shop Till You Drop Donna

Cold Critical Creature

The Commander of Attention

Poor Me Paolo

The Giant Gossip Queen

Sarcastic Push Your Buttons Beatrice

Pageant Princess Penelope

The Tough Girl

Loner Stoner

The Biggest Loser

Starving Artist

Broken Hearted Harry

Never Enough Greta

Hopeless Romantic

Nerdy Neville

Untamable Sex Beast

Chatty Kathy

Nervous Nitpicker

Queen Francesca

etc …

Keep your facets listed in your journal and add to your list as you become aware of the different sides of your personality.

2. MEDICINAL DIALOGUE (11-STEP INTEGRATIVE PROCESS)

We are going to explore *Medicinal Dialogue* together now, and by doing so, give a voice to something that has perhaps been disturbing your peace. You can use M.D. to work a dialogue with another person, money, a heavy emotion that you continuously feel, a physical disease, your Inner Child, even God or a Higher Power. This practice is limitless.

The mind may not grasp this, but when you are present in the process it will speak for itself, pun intended. I once had a client tell me that she had the most enlightening dialogue with a piece of ceramic on her kitchen counter. No joke! When you join the conversation that really needs to happen within your own Self, anything is possible. Whatever needs to be uncovered within you will project outside of you so you can see it, sometimes quite creatively. Typically, if you are attracted to someone or repelled by them, one way or the other, they carry a quality or facet that is wanting to be acknowledged and accepted within you, in honor of Wholeness.

There are two ways of using M.D. One is by hand in your journal and the other is by dialoguing vocally, which we will practice in PART III of this book together as I show you how to put all seven steps of the *Diamond Process* together.

For now, let's explore the *Medicinal Dialogue* practice through a written exercise in 11 simple steps:

1. BE PRESENT & IDENTIFY A CHALLENGE IN YOUR LIFE

First and foremost, come into the *Diamond Self* by becoming present with your body as you breathe and soften your gaze on a single still point. Once you feel connected to your inner space, choose a recent experience where you felt triggered by a person or situation.

In other words, is there a challenge in your life that you want to work through right now? Is there a specific obstacle that you are ready to overcome? Do you have a physical illness, or are you simply tired of feeling so much emotional pain?

2. WRITE DOWN THE TRIGGER YOU ARE EXPERIENCING
Write down the trigger in one sentence at the top of the page. For example: "I feel triggered because I weighed myself today and noticed I gained a few pounds despite my desire to slim down."

3. CLARIFY & WRITE DOWN WHAT EMOTION OR QUALITY IS PRESENT IN YOU
Clarify the emotion or quality that you're feeling as a result of the trigger. For example: "I feel worthless," and write it down. Notice "worthlessness" is not an emotion. Yet, it is a tangible quality, which will work for this process. You can think of this quality as one facet on a diamond. Once you clarify the emotion or quality, you have found the facet you will be dialoguing with.

4. LOCATE WHERE YOU FEEL THE EMOTION OR QUALITY IN YOUR BODY
Now, pause and let go of your pen. Close your eyes, breathe into your body, and notice if and where you feel the emotion or quality within your body. It may be isolated in one place, a general feeling all over, or you may not yet notice it in your body.

5. EXTERNALIZE THE EMOTION (GIVE THE FACET A FACE)
Keeping your eyes closed, imagine bundling all of the energy of this emotion or quality into a ball. Now place it outside of you. Imagine that this emotion or quality is sitting right in front of you, as if you have invited it over for tea. Often times, you will notice imagery arise in your mind. You may see this facet of emotion or quality as a character, color, object, shape or texture.

If it were a person, would it be masculine or feminine? How tall? What color hair and eyes? What texture skin? How old? What color shirt is he/she wearing? The key is to follow your first vision. You may see the essence of this facet immediately as an animal, person, or blob of energy, or it may be totally blank. Whatever is true for you is great. You don't have to see anything visually to utilize this practice. Trust your unique experience.

6. INVITE A DIALOGUE WITH THE FACET

From the perspective of the ***Diamond Self***, who is Aware, Authentic, and Allowing, open the space and invite a dialogue with the facet (i.e. worthlessness) you have identified.

Now that you have a good feel and possibly an image of the facet, pick up your pen and start the ***Medicinal Dialogue*** by drawing a symbol that represents your ***Diamond Self*** before writing down what you want to say or ask. A diamond shape (<>), circle, or heart shape are all great examples of symbols that help you distinguish yourself from this singular facet.

The best way to open up a dialogue is to greet the facet, ask if it has a specific name, and state the facts. It may look something like this:

<> *"Hello Worthlessness. Is it OK if I address you this way, or do you have a specific name? I felt you come up strongly today after I weighed myself and since you are here, I imagine there is something you need to share with me, or something you need from me. Is this true?"*

7. AUTHENTICALLY RESPOND FROM THE PERSPECTIVE OF THE FACET

Then, write the name of the facet (i.e. worthlessness) on the next line and let it speak. The key is to take a moment and become deeply present with the facet. Sit in it's shoes and notice how your body language changes. Inhabit its world and once a genuine response arises, write it out. The facet's response may look something like this:

Worthlessness: *"I am not worthy of a name and you could care less about me. So, why the heck are you taking the time to talk with me?"*

The key of these dialogues is ***Authenticity***. Let the facet speak it's truth. Typically, the energy that is rising up has never had a chance to express. Otherwise, it wouldn't be so uncomfortable to feel it. This is about you welcoming back a "child" that you allowed to become orphaned a long time ago. The child may be relieved, resentful, or anything in between. Your job, in the seat of the ***Diamond Self***, is to be aware of it free of judgment. Be authentic in your responses and allow it to be as it is. Remember, ***Presence*** heals!

Note: If you are dialoguing with anger, there is only one rule. Make sure that the anger is expressed outward rather than being internalized or directed at you. Our culture tends to have so much shame around anger, therefore swallowing it, which when buried long enough typically becomes toxic self-hatred. Through ***Medicinal Dialogue***, this unhealthy pattern can be transformed by allowing the anger to express in its natural direction, outwardly towards it's original and deepest trigger. In Section III, we will explore this further.

8. CONSCIOUSLY GUIDE THE DIALOGUE BY ASKING OPEN-ENDED QUESTIONS

From the seat of the *Diamond Self* (<>), simply ask open-ended questions to discover the facet. When you are responding, be authentic (this is key) and use compassionate words and inspired wisdom as much as possible. If you don't feel compassion and are triggered by the facet, then state that in an honest manner. **Authenticity** creates momentum and has the power to reveal the freeing message within the mess. For example:

<> *"I know that I should be loving and compassionate, but I feel so angry. When you come around I feel so terrible that I can't help but want you to go away."*

Let the dialogue run its course, pausing with presence between exchanges as to speak from feeling vs. thinking.

ADDRESS THESE 3 KEY QUESTIONS, WHEN IT FEELS RIGHT:
i. When and where did you first show up in my life?
ii. What have you come into my experience to teach or show me?
iii. What do you need from me?

Make sure to take responsibility for not listening in the past, trying to run or bury its need and attempts of getting your attention. The reality is that every facet has a purpose and opening up to discovering what that is has the power to birth a miracle. It may not be immediate, yet certainly over time.

9. AGREE TO TAKE ACTION ON THE FACET'S NEED YOU HAVE DISCOVERED

Once you clarify your facet's need, make an agreement to take action on that need this week. Be specific and only commit to what you will absolutely follow through with. Remember, if this were an orphaned child, you would need to be extra care-filled, ensuring that you build trust rather than creating more upset. Keeping to your agreements is how you build trust. So, only make an agreement that you can and will follow through with. Here is an example:

<> *"Is there something you need from me?"*
Worthlessness: *"Yes, I need you to accept that I am part of you. Pay attention to me. Pause with me. I need you to love me as I am."*

(Pause. **Presence**. Really taking in the request.)

<> *"I can see how I have been harsh on you, trying to get rid of you. I take full responsibility for that. I didn't even realize I was doing it. I am sorry. Is there a specific way you want me to be present with you?"*

Worthlessness: *"I would really like it if we could let go of technology and relax in nature tomorrow. I am so tired of all the doing and accomplishing."*

<> *"How about we go to the park in the morning and relax for at least thirty minutes under that beautiful oak tree before it gets too hot out?"*

Worthlessness: *"Yes. I look forward to it."*

If you become tired during the dialogue process, that is a perfect opportunity to pause, become still, and breathe. The mental chatter or attempt to "figure" things out is exhausting. This may be a sign that you are over-thinking. Simply, return to the first step: **Presence** and coming into Stillness until a response naturally arises.

10. MARK YOUR CALENDAR FOR YOUR "INTEGRATE DATE"

Once you are complete with your dialogue, and have your one action step clear (i.e. Relax under tree tomorrow morning while being present with the facet of worthlessness), crumple up the pages, let go of your pen and mark your calendar with the action step so that you ensure you follow through. Taking action allows you to integrate this facet with care.

11. PAUSE AND RESET WITH SHINE TIME

Now pause. Enjoy a few minutes of SHINE Time by placing your hands on your heart and honor yourself for taking this time to deepen in **Authenticity** and Self-Care. Once you feel ready, let the pages go safely into a fireplace, a shredder, or the trash without re-reading them. Trust in the healthy completeness of this dialogue and the Self-Trust that is now strengthening within your heart as you enjoy the one action step you committed to this week.

Note: You may prefer to keep a diary of your **Medicinal Dialogues** rather than getting rid of the pages as you write them. If so, please consider refraining from re-reading the dialogues. If inspiring insights come through that you want to remember, simply transcribe those onto a loose sheet of paper, extracting the gems and leaving behind what you have released through the dialogue.

DIAMOND SELF ACTIVATION (JOURNAL QUESTIONS)

* How do I typically communicate through challenges that arise physically, emotionally, and mentally?

* What is the easiest emotion for me to express? The most challenging?

* What is one way I can empower a healthy relationship to my most undesirable emotion today so that I mine the gems from the depths rather than getting lost in the rubble?

> "Forgiveness is a powerful force, which can release
> the past from you and you from the past.
> As you are released from the past,
> you are more available to the present."
> *Leonard Jacobson*

Week Five: Making an Offering of Forgiveness to the Past

Positive thinking and optimism have a tremendous beneficial impact on how we move through life, especially in today's world amidst countless difficulties and challenges. Yet, thinking positively will never resolve pain if we are endlessly running from it.

Many walk around in their lives with a feeling of being disempowered as they believe that the world "out there," or perhaps certain circumstances, are responsible for their unhappiness. The reality is that your outer experience is simply a reflection of your inner world over which you have total and complete dominion. The real problem exists in our perceptions. When we react to a situation without tending to the real source of the strife (our own beliefs), we lose access to the flowing fountain of **True Power** that is ever-available, becoming parched and exhausted in the process.

Earlier this year I was working with a client privately as she journeyed through the "7-Week Love-inar Program." She was in her early twenties, kind, genuine, and physically stunning. Her beauty was so pronounced that it even took me aback the first time we met. In spite of all that she had, she was tortured because of one single flaw, these dark circles underneath her eyes. She tried every kind of product to brighten her eyes, but nothing worked. Actually, some products dried out her skin, which made matters worse and resulted in an increase of anxiety in her heart.

She felt totally defeated because she couldn't find a solution, but still she could not shake the compulsion to buy every product on the market. On top of it all, she felt deep shame that this "petty" thing was so painful for her. Over the course of working together, she realized that she had a deep-seated belief that if she was not perfect physically, she would be abandoned. Therefore, if she did not get rid of the dark circles under her eyes, she would end up alone which would be devastating for her.

As we further examined her fears, she realized that if she ended up alone she might die, which is typically the core of all fear, that being the fear of death. This belief commonly develops within us unconsciously as babies, at a time when we are completely reliant on others to feed and sustain us. Here was this beautiful girl who had a caring family, and was radiantly healthy, with an abundant life, yet she could not enjoy it. This one core belief that was likely programmed into her as an infant, had turned a very beautiful life into one of suffering.

The core belief that constantly haunted her was that if she has a single flaw, she will be abandoned and die. This belief may seem outrageous to a rational, conscious, adult mind, but to the child within her who was caught up in this innocent misunderstanding long ago, the terror was very real and essential to address.

When she was a child, her mother, however loving she was at her core, emphasized to her young daughter the importance of always wearing make-up and looking perfect in public. On the occasions when friends were coming over, and she was not wearing make-up, her mother would insistently rush her off to make herself "presentable." Looking presentable became the priority over her need to be Present. As a young girl she felt pressured to leave her authentic *Diamond Self* behind in an effort to please her mom, whom she continues to dearly love.

Once we identified this core belief that was keeping her stuck (*"If I am physically flawed, I will die"*), an unraveling began to take place. With this she began to shine **Awareness** on how limited and destructive that belief had been for her. She started using

Self-Forgiveness to interrupt the pattern whenever the panic kicked in at the sight of her dark circles. Rather than spinning her wheels by shopping for concealers, she became the revealer of the beliefs that were keeping her stuck. Just as Michelangelo chiseled away at the marble, bit by tiny bit, until the angel was set free, ***Self-Forgiveness*** as it was felt and spoken, again and again, began to liberate the ***Diamond Self*** from within her.

You can also see from this example that what we believe is what we create. Although those around her loved her, with or without dark circles, she abandoned herself on a daily basis by criticizing herself and robbing herself of compassion, acceptance, and ***Presence***. One can experience no greater loneliness than being absent to their own cries for help and deepest needs.

As you can see, belief systems that are coupled with incessant thinking have the powerful ability to create our reality. They also rob us and divide our life into fragments. Repressed emotions are typically the reason we escape into the world of the mind by blaming others, shaming ourselves, or obsessing over imperfections, which is just a complicated way of avoiding what we feel. In letting go of limiting judgments, you free yourself into natural joy and make peace with who you are and what you feel. ***Forgiveness*** is how we can open the door to let the light in, just like this wise woman so powerfully demonstrated!

THE POWER OF FORGIVENESS

To be genuinely positive and present, there needs to be a willingness to overcome negative thoughts as you address everyday setbacks in a constructive, tenacious manner. With this approach you can more easily embrace the full, radiant treasure at the center of your being. If you choose no action, the same depleting re-enactment will play itself out again and again, as it continues to create an exhausting up and down cycle in you.

I realized at some point that when I obsessed over my thoughts, I became lost. Yet when I married myself to the moment, I would always arrive ***Home*** to the sanctuary of the ***Diamond Self***. When we become loyal to the ***Present Moment***, with the same devotion that you would give to a thriving marriage, life becomes amazing and filled with joy. It is extraordinary how a simple shift of focus from the thinking mind to what's right in front of you in the tangible world, including something as simple as your own breath, can have such an immediate impact.

However this begs the question, *"how do we overcome the thinking mind when it's stories can be so convincing and compelling?"* How do we create enough space and relax enough to consistently feel positive and loving toward life? One of the key ways to step into a genuine state of trust, love, and optimism in the **Present Moment** is to make peace with the past through the power of **Forgiveness**.

Reflecting on, and then correcting the fear-based belief system that has kept you in a state of fear, worry, or doubt is actually quite simple. In any given moment countless thoughts swirl in and out of our minds, which is why Awareness, as was covered in chapter nine, is essential. If we are not aware of our thoughts (as in how we react to blame and respond to praise), we miss the opportunity to untether our spirits from outer conditions.

Forgiveness is one way of not only clearing limiting beliefs, but also honoring the past and seeing yourself, others, and the choices you've made, through loving and compassionate eyes. Who you once were and the decisions you made long ago, however limited they may seem to you today, have been essential stepping-stones to awakening the treasure within. They are worthy of being honored as such.

Similarly, no matter what someone has done to you in the past, whether by holding on to resentment and negative beliefs about them or yourself, you not only keep your energy stuck in a painful past, you also limit yourself from joy and peace right now. Negative judgments and resentments are like holding onto hot coals that you're prepared to throw at whomever you despise. The only problem is that, as a result, you're the one who gets burned. **Forgiveness** is the act of dropping these white, hot coals and setting our **Diamond Hearts** free, to love bravely and full out.

Have you ever noticed that it is typically from our stumbles and "mistakes" that we learn the most, receiving the opportunity to grow stronger and wiser as a result? Even so, most of us harshly judge others, and ourselves, for our past limitations, which tends to keep us divided and cornered into a reality that is no longer relevant. This is how most people keep their treasure chest locked, by remaining stuck on the trigger. What we don't realize is that in judging ourselves or others, we block ourselves from all of the good that's available... now. All that we require is the key, and that key is **Forgiveness**.

Making an Offering to the past through **Forgiveness** is a beautiful way to reclaim lost joy and allow more love into your heart, body and life. Making an offering of for(give)ness to the past is how we give the gift of freedom to ourselves and open up the sacred.

You may be wondering, how can I give a gift to the past if it's no longer there? The truth is that in the **Present Moment**, we have the power to touch our pasts as well as our futures. This truth is easy to access when you notice how you are holding onto a negative opinion about something that happened years ago. If you become upset as you think about that past situation or person, then the past is very much alive in you now and available for resolution.

Once you identify what you have been judging harshly in yourself or others, you can then choose to forgive. *"Past self, or person from my past, I forgive and free you and in return I reclaim my life force."*
It's a conscious choice you make that's as simple as that.

One of the great gifts of moving through **Medicinal Dialogue**, by authentically expressing what you are thinking and feeling as you did in the previous chapter, is that it gives you powerful insight into the beliefs and judgments that you've been carrying. This rubble is the very "stuff" that has prevented the precious diamond that you are from shining. Embedded in your dialogues, you will discover the root judgments that have been energetically strangling your fullest potential. We will dive into this in the full seven-step **Diamond Process** practice later, in Part III of this book.

SELF-FORGIVENESS

The most essential form of **Forgiveness** is **Self-Forgiveness**. Whenever you hold resentment or negative judgment against someone, more than anything else, you're harming yourself and holding yourself back. Even if another's actions were horrific, you can choose to be kind to yourself by no longer hating them. They don't need **forgiveness**, you do. **Self-Forgiveness** is a way of surrendering the pattern of holding yourself apart from love so that you can live peacefully.

Carrying negative energy has the same effects on the body whether it is justified or not. If you realize that you've been spiraling downward by despising or judging someone, be gentle with yourself. Take refuge in the knowing that your awareness is actually good news! Now you know where your opportunity for freedom lies and because of this you know where to begin applying **Self-Forgiveness**.

Remember, this is your journey, your blossoming, and your transformation. You are the one revealing the angel that's hidden within that block of marble. This has nothing to do with anyone or anything outside of you, other than the attention they bring to the "rubble" that's been weighing you down, which has only served as your trigger. These are the essential reflections in your story that show you where to "dig" for that diamond by using the shovel of **Self-Forgiveness**.

When we were young we learned to turn "out there" for validation. However, as we awaken to the treasure within, we learn to rely on our own intentions and depth of **Presence** to assess how we are doing. With the same level of repetition, we unlearn the habit of disempowerment and lead from inner-referencing, deep listening, and love.

Love is the only worthy option and the answer is never "out there." Once you apply **Self-Forgiveness** and place an open, loving perspective before all else, you are **home** free. When this level of Self-Mastery is in place, the inevitable challenges of everyday life become gifts that strengthen your wakeful heart. When we are freed through practices like **Self-Forgiveness**, our true essence shines into the world, naturally serving as spiritual sustenance and inspiration.

TAKE A FORGIVENESS STAY-CATION

Issues and circumstances are neutral, but our perception and reaction is actually what determines whether we crumble or shine. This is where your beliefs, or rather the beliefs you picked up along the way, will be brought into the light for unpacking and examination. The reality is that every human being is doing the best they are able to in every given moment otherwise they'd do things differently, wouldn't they? By judging them or ourselves, we are wasting our energy and draining our vitality. With that simple, yet transformative wisdom, the fight drops and the heart swells with compassion as an infinite embrace of oneself and others sets in.

We are all vulnerable children of God(dess) wanting to be loved and accepted. As we lay down our defenses and surrender our hardening beliefs, a sense of humility naturally unfolds that accepts everyone, including ourselves, just as we are. Even if you are choosing not to speak to (or see someone) who hurt you, you do not have to judge or hate them. You can forgive them within your heart by forgiving yourself for harboring such a weakening judgment against them.

One ritual that my clients and I absolutely love is that of taking a *Forgiveness Stay-cation*, which is something that's especially empowering when you are feeling particularly caught in blame and upset. For a certain number of hours or days, rather than escaping your pain and everyday challenges by going away on vacation, you can **stay** present with yourself by being adamant with **Forgiveness**. Often, people go away on vacation and feel great for a week only to return *home* to "reality" and crash back down. Taking a **Forgiveness Stay-cation** helps you to find your way to *feel good* in the heart of your day-to-day life. Using the **Obstacle Clearing Statement** is especially powerful, which I'll take you through a bit later in this chapter.

Taking a **Forgiveness Stay-cation** for one week straight is often an adequate amount of time that will allow you to make a radical shift. The key to your **Forgiveness Stay-cation** is simply carving out time daily to go into deep **Forgiveness**. Thirty minutes daily, seven days in a row will suffice. Just like a needed vacation, the practice of *forgiveness* is something you do for you, freeing yourself from the stressful burden of lugging around a limiting story. The good news is that you don't have to go anywhere or spend money to experience such deep relief. Casting the burden happens within your own heart. If you are using a **Self-Nurturing Sheet** from chapter seven, you can also use it to track your progress with your **Forgiveness Stay-cation** during that week. You may even consider writing out a **Self-Forgiveness** statement at the top of the page as your own additional reminder.

A very simple **Self-Forgiveness** statement is, *"I forgive myself for judging (person's name) as _____."* For example, *"I forgive myself for judging Jack as being crass and disgusting."* Did you notice that the *forgiveness* is really aimed toward myself for having held this judgment in the first place? Again, this is not about justifying another's actions, but about empowering your choice to be free from the position of either being right or wrong. **Forgiveness** is an energetic love letter to the past, a sort of treaty and waving of the white flag that demonstrates that your freedom is more important than being right.

One of your greatest powers is in choosing to know at your core that they, just like you, are sparks of consciousness. **Forgiveness** clears your sight, allowing you to see the truth from the center of the storm even if you are the only one who chooses to stand there. Over-thinking and judging is like being caught in a hurricane... it destroys peace and refuge. **Forgiveness** protects you by bringing you right to the eye of the storm, where you are still and safe, no matter what is going on around you.

Everything in our lives is designed to awaken us and deliver us to our true *Home*, which is right here at the center of Now... a *home* beyond time and space, temporary moods, thoughts, and phenomenon. Taking a **Forgiveness Stay-cation** helps to dislodge ourselves from a variety of limiting beliefs so that we can lighten, brighten, and take flight. In doing so, we get to enjoy genuine freedom... now.

Clinging to what we believe about life, however limited it may be, might feel safe because it is familiar, but it is also keeps us blinded and entangled in suffering. **Self-Forgiveness** is a quick, effective way of using the soul-shattering beliefs that have been daily running on "repeat," to shift and evolve into your unbreakable **Diamond State**.

EVOLVING INTO OUR UNIQUE DESTINIES

In the same way that a butterfly is freed from its cocoon, or a diamond is released from the grips of heat and pressure, we are designed to break through into our full potentials and unique destinies. We are living in extraordinary times in which the evolutionary impulse is gaining momentum. Within each human heart this impulse is pushing up, as it courts us with hopes for a better world. These strong, repetitive desires for peace, freedom, and prosperity are calls from within that are asking us to return to who we already are deep within, just as "The David" rested patiently at the center of the block of marble.

By seeing the seed of the weed that has been preventing our unique destinies from flowering, we can recognize and free ourselves again and again in each given moment. I say "love your triggers," for without them you would never notice what has been keeping you small. By bravely loving what hurts within, the walls of fear relax, freeing the power and joy you are here to be.

Any time you feel negative emotion, there is clearly a limiting thought that is suffocating your life force. Migrating away from the habit of blaming others for your unhappiness and continuously recommitting to **Self-Forgiveness**, just as a star pro devotes themselves to their purpose. No matter what, this continuous recommitment is what separates those who embody their full potential and those who do not.

You can either believe that the world is to blame for your limitations and remain stuck, or you can drop the story altogether and realize that right now in this moment, you have the power to choose. You have everything that you already need within. YOU have the power to evolve. How exciting is that?

Just as the caterpillar instinctively weaves itself into the dark cocoon before there is even one single shred of evidence of a butterfly, our natural instincts are also driving us to court self-nurturing, spaciousness, and the miraculous chambers of **Stillness**. It's in these states where we regain the ability to reconnect with our innate wisdom.

However, in order to thrive and in order to awaken and evolve into our next vibrant form, we must first release the old one. If you are really tired of your painful patterns and disappointments in life, you are actually in the most fertile of conditions to bloom. Sometimes it takes being so sick and tired of the old way to awaken into the new, which is when you can ask yourself some powerful questions, beginning with:

1. "What beliefs and judgments have I been holding onto about myself and life that have kept me stuck in this pattern and out of the **Present Moment**?"
2. "How will I feel if I let go of these beliefs and judgments?"
3. "What unique destiny or higher vision is pulling me forward?"

Sitting in self-inquiry is a star-quality way to stimulate your own evolution. Yet there's a big difference between asking questions that weaken you versus questions that strengthen you. When you ask questions like, *"Why is this happening to me?"* (which contains the undercurrent of the victim), you will always receive answers that support the errant belief that you are a victim.

Instead the key is to ask empowering questions like, *"What is life teaching me through this experience?"* or *"What is my soul nudging me to bloom into as a result of my overcoming this challenge?"* or *"How can I grow from this challenge?"*

"How can I grow from this challenge?" Now, that's a star-quality question to carry around in your back pocket!

If you want to shift the things, situations, and people that you attract into your life, then change your mental programming by forgiving yourself for buying into these limiting beliefs in the first place (i.e. victim identity). From this point, consciously choose your thoughts and words. As the twelfth century Persian poet, Hafiz, once said, *"What we speak becomes the house we live in."* Using different words, you get from life what you believe in your heart and mind, whether consciously or unconsciously.

Whenever you're triggered, it is actually something for which to give thanks. Without the trigger, you would never be inclined to dig deep, notice what judgments you have been carrying around, and evolve. Every step along your journey has led you to this moment that's rich with awareness and is awakening you to your glorious, unique destiny. The fact that you are reading this book right now says that you are ready to let go and bloom. As the blessed Sadguru Shankaracharya says, "You are the good news!" You are on the fringe, actualizing the evolutionary impulse right here and right now. What could be more miraculous than that?

OBSTACLE CLEARING STATEMENT

Awakening the treasure within is more about unlearning the old than learning the new. The good news about everyday triggers is that with **Awareness** you can clearly see what's best served for you to drop. When you were born, your mind was like a clean, fresh hard drive, yet over time you learned and stored information in the same way that you save documents and ideas to your computer.

Most of what has been stored on your mental hard drive are other people's thoughts, opinions, and impressions that have been stamped on your psyche. Whatever you have witnessed, particularly prior to the age of six, before you developed the ability to filter information, is typically what has the greatest influence over you today.

Fortunately we have the power to look at our thoughts and intentionally clear the ones that have been wreaking havoc in our hearts. As soon as you are aware of a belief that has been hurting you, it begins to lose its power. One of the simple ways I enjoy freeing myself from limiting beliefs is through the use of what I call an **Obstacle Clearing Statement**. This process emerged when I was in a week-long Practicum in the desert at the end of my graduate program with the University of Santa Monica. In consciously facing the core of my soul's pain during that week, I had a significant breakthrough that left me feeling light and attuned, which spontaneously guided me to this practice.

Each afternoon during our two-hour break, I would go straight to my room, sit on my yoga mat, close my eyes, and explore the magic that was opening up for me. Something had shifted in my consciousness, which enabled me to precisely see, with 100% clarity, where I had energetic blocks in my body and the beliefs that were allowing them to remain in place.

While I had never studied Reiki or any other form of energetic healing, after some time of sitting in **Stillness**, my hands naturally began moving around my chakras (energetic centers) with intention and grace. Something miraculous was happening and it was happening through me, free of my own efforts.

As this discovery expanded, I began recalling certain memories and seeing how my perception of them had been coded in my mind, which years later had weakened my life force. With this realization I began to intentionally erase these outdated codes, or rubble, in the same way that I deleted data from my phone.

From this wide-open, intuitive perspective, my brain was no different to me than a computer. Cancel, clear, and delete were all "energetic buttons" that I could "press" to clear my own mind of limiting thoughts, which is exactly what I did. This experience proved to me that when we relax, wisdom rises and every bit of guidance that we need is given from within.

Through my history I could see that I had collected beliefs just like saving documents and I could also **choose** to erase them with intention if they were no longer needed. I also noticed that when I really **felt forgiveness**, kindness, and compassion in my heart for the part of me that took the rubble on in the first place, this technique was exponentially more powerful.

The **Obstacle Clearing Statement** (**OCS**) works best when you place one hand on your heart, one hand on your belly (or anywhere else you are guided), breathe, and ground into your body. Once you feel **Present** with yourself, say *"Anywhere I bought into the belief that _____ (you fill in the blank), I cancel, clear, and delete it and I forgive myself completely."* As you recite the statement, imagine yourself tossing that "file" (a.k.a. that old belief) into an incinerator, a trash bin, or whatever other imagery of "the garbage" works for you.

You may notice that as you recite your initial statement that another judgment arises into place, or perhaps an entire stream of beliefs will arise that no longer serve you. This is great. Keep blasting through the statement in response to the judgments that arise until you feel clear.

For example, let's say that you went to a social event and got very nervous in conversation with someone you felt romantically attracted to, or a business associate you want to work with. Maybe you judged that you spoke too much, or too little. Maybe you felt like you came off awkwardly and disempowered. You will know that there is a limiting judgment at work if you feel upset, anxious, or uncomfortable in any way.

In this example, you would say something like, "Anywhere I bought into the belief that I made an idiot of myself tonight, I cancel, clear, and delete it and I forgive myself completely." The reality is that you may have made a fool of yourself or you may not have. What I have learned through this wild thing called life is to let go of assuming altogether and to especially realize that the only person's judgment that has any power over your wellbeing is your own. You hold the key to your own destiny.

After running through that one **OCS**, notice how you feel and keep going if you need to. *"Anywhere I bought into the misunderstanding that I am not valuable unless others approve of me, I cancel, clear, and delete it and I forgive myself completely."* Let's say you rattle off a few statements and your mind kicks in saying this is too simple. This can't possibly work. Well, there you have another prime opportunity to free yourself from a limiting belief yet again. *"Anywhere I bought into the belief that transformation has to be hard, I cancel, clear, and delete it and I forgive myself completely."* If you don't feel the statement working, you may repeat it until it really sinks in. Some judgments are more deeply-seeded than others and require repetition.

When the **OCS** becomes a habit, you will start to notice negative thoughts immediately before they have a chance to affect you. It's quite freeing when the statement automatically kicks in, working its magic to clear the rubble. Although it may seem like magic, it is actually quite practical. This practice makes the unconscious conscious, which according to Carl Jung, the Swiss psychologist from the early 20th century, is the path to liberation. *"One does not become enlightened by imagining figures of light, but by making the darkness conscious."*

Whenever I am in conversation with others, I often notice their unconscious beliefs rearing themselves up through their limiting language. Just yesterday I was paying for groceries when the cashier made an error and when she caught herself she said, *"I am a master at screwing up."* Although she was kidding, the unconscious mind does not know the difference between a joke and the truth.

It's because of this that I find it equally important to use the **OCS** to avoid picking up limiting beliefs from my environment, which is when I internally say to my mind, "cancel, clear, delete." I love those three words. Not only are they fun when accompanied by three snaps: Cancel (snap), Clear (snap), Delete (snap), they also keep me conscious and awake to what my heart chooses rather than being programmed by an unconscious environment. We have the conscious power to choose what thoughts we empower and this tool is a direct, simple way of freeing ourselves in the **Present Moment**.

Whether you take a **Forgiveness Stay-cation**, or enjoy the use of those three snaps, the greatest gift we can give ourselves and others is the freedom from dysfunctional thinking. With regular use of the **Obstacle Clearing Statement**, we make a generous **Offering** to the past, and who we once were, by blessing what held us back and letting it go, thus making ourselves more available to the **Present**. Our culture can be so fixed on the future and moving forward, yet without honoring what has led up to this moment, we miss a great opportunity to align with lasting freedom and flow.

TIP FOR SUCCESS!

Just like anything else that I share in this book, please try the practices for yourself. I am not asking you to believe what I share with you. The very nature of this book, and especially this chapter, has actually been designed to help free you from beliefs. The truth is that some of these practices will work for you in a powerful manner... one will resonate today while another will support you tomorrow. Yet rather than taking my word for it, I invite you to discover, explore, and choose what works best for you.

The key is to play with the gems in this book day by day with a curious, open mind. One of the greatest offerings you can make to your past is found in letting go of rigid beliefs or expectations and having a sense of adventure today.

Stillness Heals and Illuminates Natural Energy

   I invite you to completely drop everything you have just read, trusting that whatever is in your highest good is already integrated and available when you need it. Relax your jaw, loosen your belly, soften your hips and shoulders, and simply breathe consciously into your body, bringing full awareness and energy back to yourself. For the next couple of minutes, feel free to close your eyes and empower the 3 B's: Breath, Body Awareness, Brow Center. Remember, your body benefits greatly and relaxes when you consciously breathe into it and are Present with it. Explore for yourself and when you feel complete, open your eyes and enjoy the following practice.

Your Gem Power Declaration

I am honoring, blessing, and clearing the past and awakening to the joy, ease, and abundance of today.

Diamond Self Activation
Putting it into Practice...

FORGIVENESS CARD EXERCISE:

1. Take out a sheet of paper and make a list of the most recent events that triggered you into a state of upset. Circle the event you have the most charge around.

2. Make a second list of the judgments that you were thinking about yourself, the people involved in that one event, and the judgments that you believe they thought about you.

3. Once you have all of the negative judgments listed out, take a stack of index cards (or paper cut into squares) and on one side of each index card, write your **Obstacle Clearing Statement** for one negative judgment, keeping the other side of the card blank. You will devote one card to one negative judgment and then move onto the next card.

4. Continue this exercise for one full week. Before going to bed, scan your day and track where you got triggered. List the judgments on a scrap of paper. Then, add to your stack of index cards, writing one new **Obstacle Clearing Statement** for each new card.

    For example, one of the judgments you listed may be, "*I felt like Allison was sizing me up and judging me as unattractive, low energy, and therefore worthless.*" Then, on an index card, you could say something like, *"Anywhere I bought into the belief that my value is based on how pretty I look or how vibrant my energy is, I cancel, clear, and delete it and I forgive myself completely."* Another way of saying it would be, *"Anywhere I bought into the belief that I need to impress others in order to prove my worth, I cancel, clear, and delete it and I forgive myself completely."*

    In chapter Eleven, we will be using the blank side of these very cards to further this exercise. So, keep the cards accessible, as they will come in handy for you.

DIAMOND SELF ACTIVATION (JOURNAL QUESTIONS)

* What stops me from forgiving myself and others?

* What shifts in me and my life if I forgive myself and my past completely now?

> *"Be patient toward all that is unsolved in your heart and try to love the questions themselves like locked rooms and like books that are written in a very foreign tongue. Do not seek the answers, which cannot be given you because you would not be able to live them. And the point is to live everything. Live the questions now. Perhaps you will find them gradually, without noticing it, and live along some distant day into the answer."*
> Rainer Maria Rilke

Week Six: Relaxing into Nothingness

What if I were to say to you with 100% certainly that at your core, You-Are-Nothing? How would hearing those words land in your heart? Would you hate me? Love me? Feel totally and deeply confused? Elated?

Nothing? What do you mean, NOTHING?

I will always remember hearing my spiritual teacher, Leonard Jacobson, explaining that we humans are happy to know God as everything, yet we are terrified of God as nothing. The reality is, though, God is both ... everything and nothing, the material universe and an indescribable vastness! And so are we. The most important thing that I realized that day is that I was terrified of being empty, of being Nothing. As so many of us do, my name, measurements, story, and even my pain had become my source of comfort.

Why? Well, because they are all tangible. Each one of these had become my lifesaver in the midst of a vast, bottomless ocean. However miserable I felt as a result of these aspects of my being, as long as something substantial was there I knew that I existed and somehow that brought me a feeling of safety.

If I were to let go of my "to-do lists" and plans, my story and my pain... and dig deeper than the name and picture on my driver's license... to finally break through into what is beyond all of these at my core, what would I discover? At the center of my being, I would discover nothing. Nothing? Yes literally, Nothingness, a vastness without limits, the dark void that births creation, holds it All, and dissolves every speck right back into Itself again.

The reality was that I, like most humans, had been running from this mysterious, empty, intangible God my entire life. I was desperately dodging Nothingness by chasing experiences, products, partners, and storylines that could distract me from the reality that I am swimming in a bottomless ocean without a shore. This may sound like a colossal downer, yet in reality, exploring and embracing this possibility can actually lead one to unbridled freedom.

As with most people, I realized that I'd been in an endless search, poking around in my material life for the very essence that cannot be found in any *thing*. And so long as I was running from being alone, and (shall I dare say) not the one in control, I would continue to experience this feeling of being lost. Considering that I AM, in the deepest sense of those two words, Nothing myself, I would need to learn to let go and embrace this vast Nothingness.

If this is ridiculous or confusing to you, congratulations! You are on the right track, as the mind can't possibly begin to understand any of this. If, like me, this is where you find yourself, then this is great news that can simply free your heart to rest in this vastness. In time I eventually learned to dive straight into what my mind couldn't possibly begin to grasp, which is when I took all of that running power, closed my eyes, sunk deep into the flapjack chair in the center of the retreat room, and wept.

While weeping may not seem to be very sexy or desirable, in this case it was! When you think about an orgasm or anything else deeply pleasurable, what feels so good about it is the falling away of thinking and a sort of dying into an all-consuming, floating suspense. In opening my heart to this strange, impossible-to-understand Nothingness, I grieved. I did so of all the times that I thought I knew, and all the ways in which I still hold on, as I think I know what is best for me, or for you, him or her... everyone and anyone.

Everything that I thought that I knew fell away like letters that fragmented away from words and long-winded chapters of a story that no longer belonged to me. They fell straight into a scrambled puddle of illegible tears. God *is* Nothing. I am Nothing! Eureka!

I grieved the white-bearded Santa Claus God I imagined in the sky as a little girl. I grieved the pain I thought I had to heal. I grieved my identity as a woman, as a professional, as a daughter, a sister, a leader, and a lover. I grieved my memories, my dreams, my ideas of right, and my ideas of wrong. I felt it all coming up like a cleansing geyser spewing everything out so I could breathe Nothingness in for the first time.

I Am Nothing. I know Nothing. God is Nothing.

None of it made sense, yet my soul wept, making space for what I longed for most. Truth bombs tend to burst open the flood gates which hold back the very rivers that carry us to the one ocean of our inevitable destiny. The euphoria comes once we surrender, before death, while we are still alive. Once this takes place, that's when living really begins.

When we let go, we float. It is law. And when we float, this vast, bottomless ocean is no longer something to survive or flail against. Instead it actually has our back and as we recline into it, trading a crammed mind for a brave, spacious heart, we begin to recognize and feel the **Love** that has always been there beneath the ever-present hum of the rat race. This expansive **Love** is inescapable. Whether we receive it or not remains to be seen.

When I heard Leonard's words that day and the soul chord was struck, I had to allow such unknowable emptiness to take over my body. I couldn't *think* about it. I just had to feel into what I was, all at once, both terrified to surrender to, yet hungry to remember. Such Nothingness felt daunting and infinite next to my little Veronica self with her rickety lifesaver in the middle of that infinite sea. With no reason or logic, I simply let go. For a handful of minutes, I allowed who I thought I was to die, just a little bit, into that big, scary word... Nothing.

Both within my own self and my own community, I've noticed that this is where most new agers, light-workers, and yogis tend to stop, because this is where it becomes too much. Isn't it ironic? Nothingness is too much. We want to be the best, the brightest, the most successful. We want to be everything and we surely expect that God is everything. But, nothing? No! That is too simple to comprehend.

So, we dance and dodge, recite our stories, and process our pain. All of this distraction ultimately allows us to skirt around the abyss, convinced that there is more to look at, tend to, and fix. The irony is that while there is always more to witness, there is honestly nothing to fix, and there never was. We do what we do to banish our emptiness, aloneness, and nothingness even if it means being stuck in the world's most exhausting story of all time. The ego loves drama and so long as it has you engaged in the details, it gets to continue ruling your life.

To the ego, it's terrifying to drop it all, not know, and relax into Nothing, even if for just a moment. The idea of accepting oneself completely and letting go of control is like death to the ego. Yet to the soul it's exhilarating. Stilling the mind is thrilling to the soul, while filling the mind fulfills the ego. Just like anything in nature, the ego wants to survive. It's very existence depends on thinking about a future filled with everything you want in it. It promises you a pain-free future like a carrot dangling off in the distance; you'll never reach it no matter how fast you run after it.

I myself have been a master at this sort of running, this spiritualized ego approach, which only "edges God out" of the picture. It's like saying to God, "Don't worry. I got this. I don't need your spaceship to get to the Pleiades because I have my new cross trainers! Thank you very much." The irony is that there is no "there." There is only **here** and at the deepest level of Here is Nothingness and total Silence; a Stillness so vast that everything rises out of it and dies back into it over and over again. When we can consciously surrender to Infinity, the possibilities within our lives become infinite!

GIVE IT ALL UP AND YOU WILL HAVE IT ALL

The year prior to leaving my so-called "perfect life" in Los Angeles, I kept hearing the following phrase in my head, *"Give it all up and you will have it all."* I'd heard this like a rare mating call, constant and captivating, that relentlessly howled from the jungles of mystery. "Give it all up and you will have it all." How could I do this? I was in love and thought that I had it all. Needless to say, this irritated the bejesus out of me. Why would I give up everything that I'd spent 6 years creating and building?

To say the least, this haunting mantra wasn't making the least bit of sense to me, as letting go of everything seemed to be the equivalent of death itself. As animals encoded to survive, my ego did everything to preserve me and my life as it was. Needless to say, I held on tightly as I tried everything to turn the volume up in my everyday life in an effort to drown out that irritating whisper... *"Give it all up and you will have it all."*

"Shhh," I beckoned! *"Hush now!"*

I pushed, I pulled, I covered my eyes, and plugged my ears in an effort to distract my mind. *"La la la la laaa!"* If I could just arrive at a "yes" to marriage with the man I loved and my beautifully paved life, I thought that I'd be free of this eerie, incessant voice. Yet, no matter how hard I tried, those words always seemed to catch me during moments of silence.

Yet, eventually the truth always finds her way through. In the end, the only "yes" that I needed to arrive at was a *"yes"* to completely accepting myself.

Radical Self-***Acceptance*** is full on! It is a willingness to stop running, turn within, and actually marry oneself. In hindsight, I can see that I didn't need to literally walk away from my life to "have it all." Giving it all up has more to do with surrendering the idea that outer circumstances are the source of love and joy. When we source from within, we always shine regardless of our outer conditions. This is what it means to truly have it all.

BEFRIENDING ALONENESS

Eventually, after years of twisting ourselves into the yoga postures of self-inquiry and inner-work, we ripen and mature enough spiritually. It's somewhere at this point in our journey that we approach a fork in our path. This "fork" tends to show itself in many different ways. It could be that once again we brush up against the same drama that we believed that we were beyond, or perhaps by once again experiencing the pain that we thought had been healed long ago. Yet, it could also be that we finally arrive in our dream life only to discover that we still feel unhappy.

You know you are there when the sense of powerlessness is unbearable... when you've done everything, but nothing works. This is it! This is where we get to choose between spinning our wheels even faster to avoid the void or run as fast as we can towards it and spread our wings, praying that the net actually does appear, just as the cliché preaches.

This very point along the path either awakens or dulls the soul, depending on whether you let go of the reigns or clench them tighter in an attempt to do something about this unbearable experience. I like to think of the space between the leap and the net as God. This is where you either let the Nothingness consume you, or you screech into a stop, clench your fists, and keep frittering with details as you re-enact the same old story, yet one more time. Maybe now I can find a way of making this insanity bearable. I might just be "wise enough" now to even make it fruitful. As Einstein said, *"the definition of insanity is trying the same thing over and over again expecting different results."* I couldn't agree more.

Recently, I was sitting with a friend who had reached this confronting fork in her own road. Due to a pressing and quite upsetting challenge in her life, she ended up booking four sessions with an esteemed integrative therapist. Eventually, she felt the need to confess that she had been harboring a well-concealed addiction. Just before bed every night like clockwork, she had two drinks, which for more than twenty years had been "her little secret." Once she walked her therapist through this evening ritual, she immediately realized why she was reaching for those drinks.

With her mornings *filled* and active with work, the daily "to do's," and creating with people she adored, she loved this part of her day. Yet as soon as her workday ended and nightfall struck, she found herself terrified of being alone, deafened by the silence. In the company of her nightly TV shows, and her two loneliness-softening drinks, she would eventually fall asleep to re-enact the same pattern the very next evening. The therapist had her touch the feeling of emptiness and rather than going home to drink, she was invited to get to know her aloneness as she learned to be with it, in the same way that she'd be with an old friend.

Getting to know the facet of aloneness was transformational for her. Rather than picking up a drink when she feels alone, today she gets still and makes space for the aloneness, embracing Nothingness. She has actually become intimate with who she is as "no one." Ironically, after embracing her aloneness and all the qualities she feared would lead her to being alone, she was able to romantically open herself to a man in a way that she never was able to before. Enjoying companionship from a place of wholeness is possible when we no longer need someone or something to fill the gaping hole inside. It takes becoming intimate with aloneness and embracing all the qualities (or facets) that make us feel worthless, to know and celebrate our innate worth as diamonds.

THE POWER OF ACCEPTANCE

One of the five attributes of the *Diamond Self* is *Acceptance*. This is your unconditional "yes" to yourself and to life... for better or for worse. A common setback on the spiritual path is a rejection of our more challenging facets, or sides of our personalities, that's ac companied by a habit of trying to fix or force what hurts within us out of our lives. No matter what healing technique you employ, including the Diamond Process, when you attempt to use this process to get rid of something you don't like about yourself, it won't work. The reason that relaxing into Nothingness is so powerful is because it demonstrates **Radical Acceptance** of "what is," and a brave trust in the Universe.

In **A Course in Miracles**, it's written that, *"Those who are certain of the outcome can afford to wait and wait without anxiety."* In other words, there is no need to rush, grasp, or in any way control life. When you trust in the natural order of life, and in its abundant design, you can also trust in your highest inevitable unfolding, accepting the complexity of life as it is right now.

One thing that helps me rest into this trust is investing time being a witness to nature. Creation is infinite with every single cell being one-of-a-kind. Every snowflake, leaf, sea shell, tree, human being, and beyond is one of a kind... unique. Imagine how many snowflakes have fallen through the centuries and nature continues to manifest unique, one-of-a-kind expressions. The abundance is infinite and so are we.

At some point along the spiritual path we realize that no matter what we do, something much bigger and brighter than our own efforts provides the way for us to break through into that prosperous flow. No matter how hard we relentlessly push, even when success comes, without mastering the art of **Acceptance**, we'll flop.

Contrast is an inescapable law of nature that feeds the evolutionary impulse and ensures abundance. Even so, we typically fight this inevitable cycle of life and death by pushing away pain and stalking pleasure. In the end, it is the resistance that hurts, not the contrast itself. Applying the power of **Acceptance** is how we can relax into the infinite Nothingness, soften our minds, and allow the Source of Creation Itself to reset us into the abundant expressions that we're designed to be.

SURRENDERING TO NOTHINGNESS

The ultimate gesture in honoring and awakening the **Diamond Self** is **Silence**. Incessant thinking, analyzing, and the exertion of effort only blocks the gateway between you and the **True You**. At some point, life leads us to surrender and wake up, beyond the suffering that tends to result from life's inevitable, yet temporary downs.

When we surrender the mentality of thinking, plotting, and fixing, and migrate to simply being Present with the ebbs and flows of life (in compassion, stillness, and equanimity), this is what we call "waking up." Every moment that the mind is silent, we are consciously awake.

Each time we loosen our ego's grip from the steering wheel of our life, our consciousness expands. When we simply bear witness to the story of our lives and the world around us without agenda, we free ourselves from an entanglement with it. Over time a few minutes of such sweet silence has deep, inner transformational effects.

Silence.

Stillness.

Presence.

In the silence, freedom leads and the same loving intelligence that heals a knee scrape rushes in to heal our lives. Surrendering to the **Nothingness** is the opposite of what the ego wants, as it wants to stand out. If it can't stand out through becoming successful and creating a perfect image, it will find a way to stand out through suffering and being the greatest victimized failure of all time. This is what I call feeding on the attention of "stand-in stardom."

True stardom has nothing to do with your identity. Just like the **Nothingness** at the center of everything, who you truly are is infinite, formless, and beyond measure. By strengthening the ego's habit of endlessly feeding some grand identity, as it seeks attention and publicity, we lose sight of our **True Power**, the unshakable Presence of the **Diamond Self**. At some point, there is an opportunity to let go of being ruled by your image in the world and surrendering into your true image at the center of your being... the source of your ultimate freedom.

A question that I often like to ask myself is, *"Am I OK being ordinary?"* I must admit that there are times when I very much hate the thought of being ordinary. On the other hand, my eyes well up as I remember the times in the redwoods... the most ordinary moments when I wore my frumpiest clothes as I was alone with the trees... were the most extraordinary times of my life. While I've walked the red carpet at the Academy Awards, had intimate meals with A-list stars, and have made exalted love to one of the most romantic, successful men in some of the most paradisiacal locations around the world, every one of those moments pale in comparison to my simple, authentic moments alone in the forest.

One of the great blessings of my life is that I have experienced complete opposites in my life, moving from what most would consider to be the pinnacle of posh lifestyles, to the most modest. As a result of these experiences, what I've discovered is that what really counts is how Present we are in the moment no matter where we are or who we are with. Relaxing into **Nothingness** and getting to know God and ourselves as **Nothing** is the doorway to touching Infinity and embracing everything.

Stillness Heals and Illuminates Natural Energy

    I invite you to completely drop everything you have just read, trusting that whatever is in your highest good is already integrated and available when you need it. Relax your jaw, loosen your belly, soften your hips and shoulders, and simply breathe consciously into your body, bringing full awareness and energy back to yourself. For the next couple of minutes, feel free to close your eyes and empower the 3 B's: Breath, Body Awareness, Brow Center. Remember, your body benefits greatly and relaxes when you consciously breathe into it and are Present with it. Explore for yourself and when you feel complete, open your eyes and enjoy the following practice.

Your Gem Power Declaration

I AM.

Diamond Self Activation

Putting it into Practice...

1. SHINE AND RISE:
One of the most powerful habits to create is using **SHINE Time** before you get out of bed in the morning. Rather than jumping up and immediately thinking about the day that lies ahead, I invite you to remain still for at least the first few minutes upon waking. Notice the thoughts in your mind. Feel the feelings in your body. Rather than escaping what you feel, turn into it by breathing into it. You will notice how much ease this creates. When you breathe with the feelings and let go of thinking, the body relaxes.

Allow your senses to open. Draw your awareness to the sounds outside. Are they birds singing or are they cars driving by? If keeping your eyes closed makes it easier for you to awaken the ***Diamond Self***, then do so. Yet if having your eyes open is more comfortable for you, then soften your gaze on the light coming through the window. Let your mind be full of **Nothing** as you embrace yourself and what is present in the room.

This is an especially effective practice if you are accustomed to waking up with fearful thoughts, anxiety, or depression. If so, first identify the feeling (i.e. anxiety) and then locate it in your body. Once you locate it, place your hands there and breathe into it. Be careful not to try to get rid of what you feel. Remember, the key is in accepting the feeling by simply being Present with it. I like to give the feeling permission to exist all day if it needs to. I use those more vulnerable days to be quieter and even kinder to myself.

As you breathe into the body and open up to the feeling, you will likely notice that the emotion moves to a different feeling, another location in your body, or space opens within you. Emotions are meant to move (energy-in-motion). The key here is to let it dance as you observe it with the tenderness of a mother gently cuddling her baby.

As you practice this over time, you will notice that your body will relax, your mind will bloom into peace, and you will start your day centered and grounded... even before you get out of bed. Rather than "rise and shine," enjoy **SHINE Time** and then rise. Explore and enjoy the benefits. With daily repetition, over time they'll grow.

2. SAVASANA:

Savasana is the final resting posture in yoga. As one of the most replenishing postures, it allows all of the benefits from the active postures to assimilate. In Sanskrit, Savasana means "corpse pose," which consists of laying flat on your back, fully surrendered and still.

In the first few months of my time in the redwoods, I was not only processing my emotions and crying (hard) daily, I was also playing the title role in the mythological play, "Eurydice." With several costume changes, and no intermission, I was in every scene, except for one. For ninety minutes straight, four nights a week (and without a moment to spare), I gave everything that I had within me.

On one particular day, I had grieved so deeply that my energy was completely gone. My eyes were swollen and my body ached... and I still had to be on stage that night. Knowing that nature provides the greatest form of emotional recharge, I headed to the bluffs along the ocean where I would rest and breathe for an hour. As I laid in Savasana on the flat rocks, beneath the warm sun and above the crashing waves, I spontaneously envisioned that I was on my last few breaths of life. That day, I felt so weak that this didn't require much imagination. I was totally empty.

As I surrendered my body fully in this corpse pose, I wondered what I would regret about my life if these were, in fact, my final moments. I was surprised to discover that the only thing I yearned to change was the fact that I had not been present for much of my life. From my perspective on the rocks, the sky was breathtakingly blue and the sun was palpably loving. The striving and fighting were over. For once I could see clearly and everything looked so alive. The sounds of the sea provided sheer healing magic and the birds were like miracles beaming through the sky. I could now see life crisply and my goddess, was she beautiful!

This courageous practice of dissolving into **Nothingness** led to the **North Star Intention** for my life today, as well as the writing of this book. In exploring death, I found life. It was right there in front of me all along. It is amazing what can arise out of relaxing into **Nothingness**, letting go, and embracing the mantra of, *"I don't know."*

To practice this corpse pose meditation, simply lay flat on your back on the floor or on the ground out in nature with your arms and legs long and straight. Get comfortable as you completely let go of any effort. Let yourself imagine that you are on your last few breaths of life and your body is limp. What does it feel like to have no story, no name, no job, no relationship, no anything? That's right... Nothing! Is there anything in your life, from this perspective, that you would have liked to have done differently?

Allow yourself to relax into this space and notice what comes up mentally, physically, and emotionally. The key is to let yourself soften and fall away from thinking. Once you feel complete, take a few deeper breaths, then write in your journal in free-form, from your present moment stream of consciousness.

   I. **What was the greatest realization for you?**
   II. **What did you enjoy most about this Savasana?**

3. I AM NOTHING. I AM EVERYTHING:

Contemplate this quote: *"Wisdom tells me that I am nothing. Love tells me that I am everything. Between the two, my life flows."* ~Nisargadatta Maharaj

DIAMOND SELF ACTIVATION (JOURNAL QUESTIONS)

* Who are you without your story?

* How would your life be different if you gave yourself permission to be ordinary?

* Is there anywhere in your life that you are attached to being the best, hindering your ability to enjoy where you are?

* Is there anywhere in your life where you play a victim or pretend to be limited? What do you gain from this?

* How does it feel to consider the reality that you are Infinite now and there is nothing that needs to change in the future to get somewhere worthwhile?

* What does Nothingness feel like to you in your body?

> "It is not in the stars to **hold our destiny,
> but in ourselves.**"
> *William Shakespeare*

Week Seven: Declaring Your Destiny

I will always remember one of my lowest lows, which believe it or not, took place ***after*** my confronting months of solitude in the redwoods. Upon returning to Los Angeles to be with my beloved, Jason, I was working three jobs, including running my own business, which required everything that I had within me. Instantly I went from 0 to 100 miles an hour and it took its toll. Some of those mornings I woke up shaking so hard at the thought of my day ahead, that I could barely drink a glass of water without spilling it. After a year and a half of living in pristine Nature, the pace of a major city was a real shock to my system. Everything I had discovered in the redwoods felt like it was slipping away beneath the frenzy necessary to simply survive.

At the time Jason and I had just begun living together in a tiny studio apartment. My body was depleted and I felt like life was whipping me around ruthlessly. To complicate matters more, I was in debt. I couldn't understand how I could feel so powerful and connected during meditation, yet as soon as I entered the world, I felt like an ant trapped in a jar. In this vulnerable state, I began reflecting on the luxurious life with my ex-boyfriend that I'd left behind. I couldn't believe that I'd traded a queen's life for what felt like the life of a beggar. I also began to wonder if all of the growth that I'd experienced in the redwoods was worthwhile? More importantly, I began to wonder if my new life with Jason was really worth it? Although I was deeply in love and making a meaningful contribution to others, I was also getting cooked by metropolitan living. As a result, my faith was suffering the most.

Everyday I woke up and thought about getting in my car and returning to those woods, yet everyday I chose to stay in this new, yet spartan, setting. Deep down, I knew that everything that had awakened in me was worthless unless I could embody it in the world. One of my bosses at the time told me a story about Zen monks who live in the high mountains of Japan. Once they reached satori, or enlightenment, the Zen master would say, "Good!" and then send them off to Tokyo of all places. I kept that story close to heart and even though I wished it were not true, I knew that staying in LA was part of my soul's curriculum. The City of Angels still had a lot more to teach me.

If the redwoods were my second Masters program, returning to Los Angeles was my Doctorate. Somehow giving up my old life made sense in the redwoods, while in the city I was haunted by the thought that I had made a colossal mistake. I felt like I was standing at the base of Mount Everest, being asked to climb it with no equipment or supplies. It felt impossible.

The greatest challenge of this was living in such a small space with the man that I love, as there was no place for me to hide. Day after day I stood before him emotionally, psychologically, spiritually, and physically bare... completely exposed as the person I had become. There was no way to be in my safe zone by temporarily putting on a perfect image, as I'd done for so long in my past. Every abandonment issue that I didn't even know about came rising to the surface. As a result, he was seeing me at my worst and I hated it. Yet in spite of all of my fears, insecurities, and near zero level of energy, he still loved me. As often as I thought about leaving, I simultaneously expected him to say, *"You know what, I didn't sign up for this. Maybe you should go back."* Instead, he stood by me compassionately and patiently in a solid reflection of how I was actually showing up for me.

During that time, I remained devoted to using the **Diamond Process**. Although, I did not have the privacy to talk through the Medicinal Dialogues,

I did have my **Diamond Process** journal. Every morning, I woke up as early as I needed to, sat outside with a cup of tea, a pen, and my journal, and poured everything out onto the page. In doing so, I gave a voice to my fears and doubts, especially the wounded child within me that felt like she was carrying the world on her back... and all she really wanted was to go back "home" to be with the trees. My inner child was terrified, waiting for Jason to leave as it seemed that my little girl was being way too much for anyone I'd known in the past to handle.

Her greatest fear was that she'd end up down and out just like her mother. This was the real monster... the fear deep inside me that reared it's ugly head every chance that it could. As my mind weighed heavily with fear, my heart grew weary. Thankfully, I had the ever-welcoming, white, open pages of my journal to turn to each morning as my sanctuary. On some level, I was learning to re-parent myself, as I listened intently to little Veronica's fears... loving her through it all.

On one of my tougher mornings, I opened my thick red journal which was nearly full and confessed to D (the nickname for my **Diamond Self**) that I felt like LA was swallowing me. I was drowning in negative thinking and pleaded for guidance.

I paused and relaxed into my breath, patiently awaiting D's response. At first as I held the journal to my heart with my eyes closed, there was nothing but silence. I could feel my heart beating and the sound of the leaves rustling on the trees. D had nothing but love and compassion for me which I felt from the inside, a sharp contrast to the drama in my mind. Eventually though, the following words slowly and gently flowed like honey from my pen onto the page.

Dear One,
You are powerful. You simply learned to feel powerless. You are Love. You simply learned fear. You are innately valuable. You simply learned that you have to earn your worth. As easily as you learned these misunderstandings, you are now unlearning them.

Every step, stumble, and fall along your journey, including this one, is teaching you to rise and stand firmly as the authentic you through anything. You are a star. A real one. The kind that lights up the sky. There will come a time, when you will be established in who you truly are, my love, beneath the inevitable fluctuations. Be patient. This process is gradual.

Just remember that the Light that lights up the world lives right at the center of your heart. Think with your heart. Speak from your heart. Words are powerful. Use them as vehicles of gratitude. Witness the fearful thoughts and remember, they are not you, nor are they true. Like a toddler exploring your boundaries, the ego will push, tug, and do what it does until you make this moment your throne just like the Queen of the Forest. Remember? The concrete jungle is no different. You were designed to shine anywhere.

Consider this love letter your divine invitation to declare your destiny. You know how, sweetheart. Simply, let Love lead you in thought, word, and deed, moment by moment. Keep returning to this question:

What does your heart say?

Love,

D.

I closed the journal, and my eyes, placed both hands over my heart, and spontaneously went deep into Self-Forgiveness.

I forgive myself for buying into the misunderstanding that I am weak.
I forgive myself for judging myself as destined to fail.
I forgive myself for buying into the belief that I am powerless.
I forgive myself for judging myself as incapable and worthless.
I forgive myself for buying into the belief that my best years are behind me.

I kept going until nothing remained to be forgiven. Yet again, I had to clear the rubble so that I could make space for Love. Then I paused for a deep breath before declaring my destiny, just as D had suggested, from my heart.

The truth is everyday I am remembering who I really am more and more.
The truth is that it's not always easy, yet I am becoming braver and more masterful with self-kindness everyday.
The truth is my true value can never be created or destroyed. It just is.
The truth is I am lovable just as I am.
The truth is I am fully capable of finding my way through this.
The truth is I am growing at a rapid pace in the face of my greatest fears.
The truth is I can feel the wounded child within me and it is a privilege to hear her and love her.
The truth is I am learning the art of unconditional love.
The truth is I have a powerful soul on a pure mission of total freedom.
The truth is with patience and perseverance I can create a wealthy, healthy, beautiful life.
The truth is I am a blessing to Jason and those I share myself with.
The truth is the best time of my life is right now and only gets better as I love myself more.

The truth is I am being initiated into radical compassion allowing me to serve more purely.
The truth is I am the strongest woman I know and I am grateful to be me.
The truth is I am worthy of joy, peace, and abundance.
The truth is that in accepting and trusting where I am now, I am allowing myself to bloom.
The truth is I am blooming and grateful for this soul-growth spurt.
The truth is I am absolutely amazing.
The truth is I am genuinely remembering how magnificent I am.
The truth is I really don't know anything. I only know that God is love and God produced me. Therefore, I am love.
The truth is I AM LOVE.
The truth is I am valuable.
The truth is I am worthy.
The truth is that true power lives within me and is independent of outer circumstances.
The truth is I am the way. I am the power. I am the light that lights up every room.
The truth is I am infinite. Wheweeee!
The truth is I CAN. I AM. I HAVE. I CAN. I AM. I HAVE. I CAN. I AM. I HAVE.

I kept going until I became so giddy and at peace inside that the story of my life no longer had a hold on me. Actually, I forgot about it. As a result, all that was left was a sense of pure power, joy, and appreciation for the moment. The words that I'd used completely shifted me. They weren't just words or wishful thinking muttered to escape the pain. They were soulful declarations of appreciation that I could feel with my heart. I was declaring my destiny! When D asked me, *"What does your heart say?"* my perspective shifted from the lies that I'd bought into (i.e. there is something wrong with me, or that I am powerless) to the truth. This is the power of using conscious language to pivot your focus and declare your destiny through the power that's held within the spoken word.

HOW TO DECLARE YOUR UNIQUE DESTINY

Words are powerful. Depending on what we say and why we are saying it, they can either hurt us or heal us. I use the above example to demonstrate how being present with yourself through a breakdown can lead to a breakthrough, by speaking to yourself using words that are Self-Loving in nature. That morning I went into work feeling stronger and the little girl within me finally felt safe. While my circumstances didn't change, I did. The reality is, if I am lost in fear and negative self-talk (which originates from the wounded child), I cannot stand strong as a balanced **Presence**... or as my functional inner parent or mother. Often, we become so identified with fear that we don't realize that we're simply taking a trip into the inner child's world, and to free ourselves from it, all our wounded child really needs from us is stability, compassion, and radical acceptance.

Living in LA where my outer conditions initially made me shake, I eventually learned to be a pillar of **Love**, **Devotion**, and **Trust** for myself no matter what. I became masterful at shifting my attention from all the dramas that pulled me off center, placing it back into my body, heart, and soul. By putting Self-Love first, even if it meant losing my job, reputation, or for that matter, my relationship, I became the safe haven that I'd once believed I would find somewhere "out there."

Declaring your destiny has everything to do with remembering that you are powerful. Your thoughts are powerful. Your words are powerful. You and God, Spirit, The Universe... whatever you choose to call It (with a capital "I"), are collaborating in every moment. You are an active participant in sculpting your destiny. If you speak words of self-respect, life will reflect that back to you. If you use words of peace, your world will be one of peace. The very thoughts you empower and words you speak are literally shaping your world. So, the question becomes what world do you choose to live in... one filled with fear or one filled with love? Do you choose a world where you have to fit in to feel valuable, or do you base your worth on how authentic and present you are? In this world, which part of you leads... your ego or your heart?

Every time you imagine something repetitively and feel it intensely, you are creating a magnetic vibration that attracts that very frequency back to you. For example, if you are in despair because you are tired of being alone and you are constantly thinking about how bad it is to be single, you will likely attract more misery and loneliness.

On the other hand, if you are consistent with Self-Love on good days and bad days, enjoying your life alone, and at the same time are open to sharing your life with someone, you will most likely attract someone with whom you can authentically enjoy life with. What you want may not come in the exact form that you imagine, but it always comes in the way that is best for your soul. Declaring your destiny has everything to do with what you are thinking, speaking, and feeling about yourself. Are you thinking about what is missing in your life or are you grateful for what you have now? Are you focused on the problem or are you choosing to be the solution? In other words, you have the power to declare your destiny by being crystal clear about the object of your repeated focus and live in that vibration now. Vibe **with** your vision and positive change is bound to take shape.

If this were easy everyone would be thinking good thoughts as they lived authentically and freely all the time. However, after a lifetime of establishing the patterns of harboring our learned untruths, and fostering our limiting interpretations of reality, we begin by creating an inspiring lifestyle, which sets the stage for our continued unlearning. With our old ways of thinking unlearned, it's much easier to begin using our minds in a continuously positive and loving manner.

UNLEARNING FEAR AND DECLARING YOUR DESTINY OF LOVE

Declaring your destiny is about taking the very lies you have discovered you have been telling yourself and turning them around... and in the process, powerfully turning your life around.

Again, as the great mystic Hafiz shared so eloquently, *"The words we speak become the house we live in."* Your thoughts and words are building your life.

In the practice section of this chapter, we will be using your own forgiveness statements to create declarations of truth to consciously rebuild your life with love. First, though, let's explore the keys to declaring your destiny.

FOUR KEYS TO DECLARING YOUR DESTINY:

1. **Realize that you are a powerful co-creator.** If there is anywhere within your mind that you believe you are powerless or a victim, this is an opportunity to go back to the practice in Step 5, releasing this limiting belief (rubble) from your consciousness. Many of us have learned within society that there is some big, punitive God in the sky who, in much the same manner as "Santa Claus," is tracking whether we are naughty or nice. We learned that the power is outside of us and that it is blasphemous to even believe in your own divinity. Yet when you look at the core of every religion, they all point us to God, the Creator, being within.

For example:
Christianity says, "The kingdom of heaven is within."
Buddhism says, "Look within. You are the Buddha."
Hinduism says, "God dwells within you as you."

It's with this understanding that you get to return to the brilliant, playful child within you, your Inner Essence, who came into this world innocent, bright-eyed, and ready to co-create from the heart.

2. Release lower thoughts so you can live your Higher Destiny. The reason I saved "declaring your destiny" as the final step is because it is not possible to genuinely feel optimistic about your future when repressed, negative emotions from your past are weighing you down. The **Diamond Process** journey is designed to help free you from limitations and blocks so that you naturally bloom into light-hearted **Presence**.

Note: If you are using positive thoughts and words to escape your current reality, declaring your destiny will not work. Positive thinking will just be another form of masking pain. With that said, though, you can choose an honest, loving thought that brings you one step closer to your Higher Destiny.

For example, when you feel upset, declaring "I am joyful" will feel as ridiculous as calling your dog a kitten. No matter how many times you think it, the dog is still a dog. Yet, what may feel true in the face of upset could be something like, *"I am willing to allow this feeling of upset to exist right now. I may not like it, but it's okay. I am learning to be more gentle and compassionate with myself. I still love and accept myself as I am."* Can you feel the lightness of this way of thinking?

3. Choose your words wisely. In addition to the power of your thoughts, your words also powerfully inform your reality. In fact, there's an entire school of thought on this very subject that's known as, "Conscious Language." I believe that this is a topic worthy of your attention. I would recommend that you read more about it if it resonates for you.

I once took a course on this subject that was facilitated by a dear friend and colleague, Shirly Joy Weiss. It was a game-changer for me. When you begin to look at words and their deeper meaning, it becomes easy to see why we attract what we attract. Look at the word "inform," in-form. Your words bring things into form. Just like we plug in-form-ation into Google in order to find what we are looking for, the words you speak will take you to a certain destiny.

If you keep complaining about how terrible your boss is or how much you hate your body, I assure you that your reality will make sure that you get more reasons to complain about your boss and shame your body. If you speak genuine words of appreciation, inspiration, and love, you will attract more and more to celebrate. If you often say, "I have to do this," or "I have to do that," there is a sense of powerlessness, as if you don't have a choice.

Notice the energetic difference in these three ways of saying the same thing: 1. I have to go to this work function tonight. 2. There's a work function tonight that I'm going to. 3. I choose to go to this work function tonight. Notice that the first one is negative in nature, while the second one is benign. Yet, the third one is positively reinforcing.

This is an opportunity to become crystal clear with your words and let your language reflect the powerful creator that you are.

4. Be in a state of Appreciation now. Gratitude is the fast track to building a beautiful destiny. Appreciation is one of the attributes of the *Diamond Self* and, in and of itself, has the power to transform your life. No matter where you are on your journey, whether a great high or the darkest low, there is always, and I mean ALWAYS, something to appreciate.

On a personal note, today I received one of the most difficult emails I have ever received from someone I dearly love. So, I lit a candle, threw two pillows down on the ground and worked the full *Diamond Process* (as you will learn how to do in the next section). By the end I was so grateful for the trigger (this person's harshness) for helping me see a core limiting belief that I was unaware of carrying. That person was just reflecting the lie I had been believing about myself that was keeping me stuck. Feeling the pain of this person's judgment opened my awareness, which led me to drop the "rubble" and step more bravely into my authentic destiny, whether they agree with it or not.

It is easy and important to be thankful for what we love. Yet it's even more important for you to appreciate the very challenges that have made your skin curl. These very triggers have brought you the awareness that's necessary for you to be able to choose the treasure. Within them lies the potential to lead you to True Power, being able to love yourself through anything, and to radically accept yourself regardless of outer circumstances.

As you can see, there is always an object for your gratitude, with little things being especially important to acknowledge. If you have eaten food today, you have something to appreciate. If you have access to empowering material like this book, you have something to appreciate. If you have a safe place to rest your head at night, you have something to appreciate. When we open our eyes with gratitude to the little things we have, we align with our **Diamond Selves**. If you are not grateful now, what makes you think you will be grateful when you have something different? I can assure you, as you know from my personal story, that the only time you can be happy is now and it has very little to do with how blessed you are materially. Don't get me wrong, it is great to have a beautiful life and it is even greater to love and appreciate your life no matter what you have or own.

To activate the super power of Appreciation, simply think thoughts and speak words of Appreciation with feeling for what is already in your life. This isn't about faking it. This is about constantly looking for what you appreciate and voicing it to yourself and to others. Gratitude for what you have now can move mountains, clearing the way for even more to be thankful for as your destiny unfolds.

Stillness Heals and Illuminates Natural Energy

    I invite you to completely drop everything you have just read, trusting that whatever is in your highest good is already integrated and available when you need it. Relax your jaw, loosen your belly, soften your hips and shoulders, and simply breathe consciously into your body, bringing full awareness and energy back to yourself. For the next couple of minutes, feel free to close your eyes and empower the 3 B's: Breath, Body Awareness, Brow Center. Remember, your body benefits greatly and relaxes when you consciously breathe into it and are Present with it. Explore for yourself and when you feel complete, open your eyes and enjoy the following practice.

Your Gem Power Declaration

I AM grateful for my ever-blooming life.

Diamond Self Activation

Putting it into Practice...

1. HEART MANTRA

During a time of great healing, near the end of my time in the redwoods, I realized that I had a choice. I could either stay in the dark, or I could crawl my way out, bouncing out of the lies, which to that point, I'd been telling myself. Needless to say it was a painful time that was also simultaneously **empowering. Although, staying** on the ground and giving up would have **been easier,** I began praying for help.

Almost immediately, with my eyes closed, I saw an image of a newborn baby that landed in my imagination like an email dropping into an inbox. It was effortless and just as easy as watching a movie. This baby was on a cold marble floor, without a bit of warmth around her... no hand to hold and not a soul to protect her. She was so pure, gentle, and perfect, which moved my heart to tears as I realized that this baby was me. She was the seed of my existence, and it was up to me to rescue her, return to the light, and make a new choice.

This was when I found my heart mantra. As I cradled myself in tears that day, feeling an embrace that no other human being could have ever matched or provided, I digested my own loving as four words rose from within me. Like bubbles rising from an ocean floor, these words slowly found their way up through my solar plexus, past my heart, into the long corridor of my throat, then finally tumbled from my salty lips...

I LOVE MY SOUL!

The love I felt for myself was indescribable. It is what I imagine God must feel for all of us. There was no sense of ownership or conditions, just love... Divine love. I could see my own preciousness and the purity of this Self-Love transformed the way that I looked at myself. I share this story as a seed for you to declare this level of self-love and explore what your own heart mantra may be.

Take a moment now and place one hand over your heart and the other over your belly. Close your eyes and breathe into your soul, into a deeper place within you that is beyond logic. Then whisper to yourself, "What is my heart mantra?" Listen patiently and stay with your breath. Trust your intuition. If nothing comes, simply enjoy the SHINE Time. If a clear mantra arises, give thanks for it and enjoy reciting it regularly with a loving embrace. You may notice that it changes over time as you bloom.

2. DECLARATIONS OF TRUTH

Declarations of Truth are a form of re-scripting your life, using the negative judgments and forgiveness statements from the "Putting it into Practice" section at the very end of chapter 11 (Forgiveness Card Exercise) to pivot your course by turning them around. Here are some examples of Declarations of Truth:

The Truth is I AM designed to thrive.
The Truth is I AM worthy of living a great life.
The Truth is I AM precious, powerful, and infinite with potential.

Now that you can see the negative beliefs that have been running you (from the Forgiveness Card Exercise at the end of chapter 11), you are simultaneously getting clarity on how to map your Declarations of Truth. With these you can consciously declare your love-filled destiny by connecting to your heart and using conscious, constructive language to build your destiny.

For example, if your judgments and forgiveness statements from the Forgiveness Card Exercise were around lack or unworthiness, then you can turn your life around into Plentitude and Self-worth. Thank Goddess for those judgments, for they are showing you the doorway to resurrecting the Truth!

If your judgments were around confusion, or suffering, then you can turn your life around to clarity and peace. If your judgments were around self-pity or fear, then guess what? You can turn your life around with declarations of self-confidence and love. If your judgments were around feeling lost or alone, then you can turn your life around to being awake and residing in a state of Oneness with all of life. It is entirely up to you. Holding a weakening or an empowering perspective is simply a choice - your choice! Can you allow the darker feelings to exist, rooting down in acceptance and compassion, while choosing to open up to love? I believe that you can... actually, I KNOW that you can.

Remember! You don't need to know the "how," just the "what." With that said, take a look at the Forgiveness Cards (index cards) you made during the "Putting it into Practice" section in chapter 11. On one side of the card is your forgiveness statement and the other side of the card is blank. Space was made within you already through the Self-Forgiveness exercise. Now, is your chance to write your Declarations of Truth on the blank side of each card, and thus write the program for your destiny.

Simply take the limiting belief that you have forgiven yourself for holding and turn it around. For example, if your Forgiveness Statement was "I forgive myself for buying into the misinterpretation of reality that I will never have enough because I am not enough," you can turn it around to the positive. I AM enough, here and now.

Using the words I AM is a great place to start. As mentioned earlier in this book, the words "I AM" are powerful. They not only encapsulate the deepest truth of who you are, but any words you put after them literally craft your identity. We're talking super-potency here!

Here are some more examples of Declarations of Truth:
The truth is I AM designed to thrive.
The truth is I AM choosing to thrive.
The truth is I AM Radiant.
The truth is I AM Worthy.
The truth is I AM Valuable, just as I Am.
The truth is I AM a gift. My Presence is a gift.
The truth is I AM loving who I AM, more and more everyday.

If all of this feels unnatural, then simply set the intention to see yourself and your life through the eyes of Source, of Truth! With time, you will discover beyond the layers of misunderstanding and thinking, how utterly Lovable you are!

If your level of Self-Acceptance and heart-centered desire to be whole is strong enough, you can declare your destiny. You just have to desire to be free and be congruent in your words and actions. These declarations of Truth, are your way of choosing and actualizing your creative birthright to author your own life by making peace with the past and pulling that angel out of the marble today!

Once all of your cards are complete, keep them in a stack in your Space of

Love with the Declarations of Truth facing upward. Keep creating new cards each time you hit up against rubble and enjoy the art of declaring your destiny by reading your Declarations of Truth out loud regularly!

3. WEAR YOUR CROWN OF GRATITUDE

Even if you are desperate to have something occur in your life within a certain time frame, you are more likely to experience it at some point if you enter into the feeling that you need nothing to change. This is the great paradox of declaring your destiny. Simply, appreciate what you have now, while allowing yourself to dream from your heart.

A fun way to do this is to put on an invisible crown of gratitude each day before you walk out the door. This is your "crown of gratitude." You may even wear an actual crown made of flowers or gemstones if it inspires you. Let this invisible or actual crown empower you to look for what you are thankful for throughout your day. As you play with this perspective of being focused on what you appreciate now, you just might find yourself matching up with a destiny fit for a queen (or king).

DIAMOND SELF ACTIVATION (JOURNAL QUESTIONS)

* If you could write one sentence to describe your ideal destiny, what would it be?

* What is the biggest limiting belief that has held you back for most of your life? What is the turnaround Declaration of Truth statement?

* What is one quality you embody more of in your ideal destiny?

* What is one thing you already have in your life today that matches your ideal destiny?

PART THREE
THE DIAMOND PROCESS

Chapter 14 - The Seven-Step Transformational Process in Action

Chapter 15 - Lead Your Life With Love

> "Many of us spend our whole lives running from feeling with the mistaken belief that you **cannot bear the pain**. But you have already borne the pain. **What you have not done is feel who you are beyond that pain.**"
> — Kahlil Gibran

The 7-Step Transformational Process In Action

Welcome to the complete **Diamond Process**, the 7-step transformational technology that's been designed to support you in using your everyday triggers to awaken the treasure within.

As a result of this journey you have been steadily migrating away from living in your mind due to over-thinking, into being more focused and present in the heart of Now. Through observing your breath and opening to your body's senses, you have also learned to relax. Additionally I have led you to explore the power of Intention and how having a **North Star Intention** keeps you on track with your soul's purpose.

You've also learned how to expand your Awareness as you noticed which of your triggers pull you off your path. Armed with Awareness you've now discovered how you can use the tools of **Forgiveness**, **Medicinal Dialogue**, and **Flow Journals** to return to the **Diamond Self**. You've also discovered the importance of emphasizing the magic wand of **Radical Self-Acceptance**, which empowers you to drop your draining agendas to fix and fight "what is." As well, I led you on an adventure into Nothingness, where you learned to surrender your story and touch your infinite nature before declaring your own unique destiny.

In celebration, to this point you've learned a lot and done a lot of very good work. However, as a result of working the 7-Step *Diamond Process*, you'll discover an even greater gift within.

THE PURPOSE OF THE 7-STEP DIAMOND PROCESS

Now that you have used each step as an individual gem, you are prepared to use all 7 steps together as you constructively move through a specific challenge that has thrown you off center. This process is especially beneficial when emotion is surging through your body. If you can feel a strong feeling in your body, then it is active through your body in the **present moment**, rather than in your mind. While the process can certainly be used to explore and discover on a more mental level, the transformational nature of this process is most effective when your emotional energy is up.

The reason the *Diamond Process* works so effectively is in its ability to support you in expressing what has been repressed, while also engaging you in the art of listening as you become genuinely Present for yourself. Oftentimes, physical sickness is nothing more than toxicity stored in the tissues that needs to be relieved. Under normal healthy conditions, the body naturally releases any beginnings of sickness from the body, which is the main reason why relaxing and reducing your level of stress is so critical.

However, the biggest challenge is in understanding that the beginning stages of healing can sometimes seem to get worse just before it gets better. Yet, because we live in a culture that typically chooses a pill to relieve the symptom, as opposed to choosing lasting and genuine healing, as soon as discomfort arises and a pill is taken (or an addiction is favored), the toxicity retreats back into the tissues. This simply prevents a true healing, which applies to emotional healing as well. When emotions are repressed they tend to retreat back into the emotional body until the next triggering event, or opportunity for lasting healing, takes place.

An important aspect of the *Diamond Process* is that it's also been designed to expand one's abilities to let go of resistance and be present with their discomfort, one dialogue at a time. Transformation is the natural byproduct of feeling and expressing pain while listening with love and compassion, rather than running with fear to a quick fix that doesn't actually heal the root issue.

Insanity has been defined as doing the same thing over and over again, expecting a different result. With the 7-Step **Diamond Process**, you now have an opportunity to try something that's new, empowering, and liberating! In reality, you could easily consider this process to be a form of inner-yoga, or even an inner-counseling, that will help you return home to your **Diamond Self**. Whether someone pissed you off, your health is challenged, or you are tired of being in a state of financial, romantic, or other form of lack, you can use this process to make peace within yourself as you claim the gems that are available beneath the rubble.

Keep in mind that you can always use one of the steps as a stand-alone gem depending on your own specific need in the **present moment**. For example, the second step of Intention can be used on it's own every morning to start your day. You may also get something off of your chest by using the tool of free form writing from the fourth step of **Medicinal Dialogue**.

Yet, by moving fully into this 7-Step System, you'll engage a state of consciousness, purposefulness, and power that can take your inner-resourcefulness and freedom to the next level.

What follows is a brief overview of the process.

DIAMOND, an acronym which defines this 7 Step process, stands for:

1. **D**iamond Self

2. **I**ntention

3. **A**wareness

4. **M**edicinal Dialogue

5. **O**fferings of Self Forgiveness

6. **N**o-thing-ness

7. **D**eclaration Statements

The purpose of the **Diamond Process** is to be in the **Present Moment** as much as possible so that we can enjoy our lives, access our full potential, and be in a state of **True Power**. We all know how to use our minds to think, plan, and often times worry. However the intention of the **Diamond Process** is to awaken our hearts and pivot us from the "hell of self-consciousness," to the super power of **Self-Awareness**. By becoming more aware, we go from overthinking and getting lost in others to being self-expressed and in a transformational state of Love, which begins with Self-Love.

5 KEYS FOR MAXIMIZING YOUR DIAMOND PROCESS SESSION

1. Presence is PRIMARY! Remember, this is your opportunity to be with, stay with, and compassionately see yourself through anything. Bring sacred pauses to this process by periodically taking a few deep breaths. Remind the **Present Moment** that you are still here with it by moving from your mind's agenda to how you are feeling in your body. Although you are triggered about something that happened in the past, or are worried about the future, you have the power to breathe into what you are feeling in this moment as you activate the **Diamond Self** and honor the *"Here and Now!"* This **Present Moment Awareness** will also support your clarity and connect you with your inner wisdom, which will guide your **Diamond Process** session. Allow the tangible *present moment*, and the truth of the *present moment*, to be your foundation for this process.

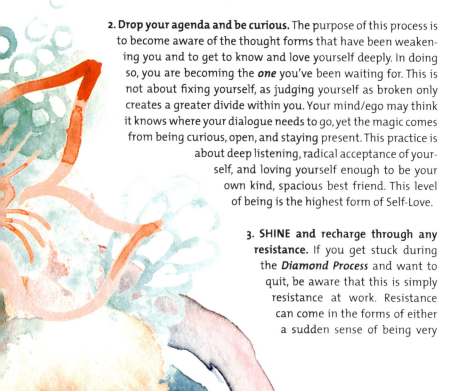

2. Drop your agenda and be curious. The purpose of this process is to become aware of the thought forms that have been weakening you and to get to know and love yourself deeply. In doing so, you are becoming the *one* you've been waiting for. This is not about fixing yourself, as judging yourself as broken only creates a greater divide within you. Your mind/ego may think it knows where your dialogue needs to go, yet the magic comes from being curious, open, and staying present. This practice is about deep listening, radical acceptance of yourself, and loving yourself enough to be your own kind, spacious best friend. This level of being is the highest form of Self-Love.

3. SHINE and recharge through any resistance. If you get stuck during the **Diamond Process** and want to quit, be aware that this is simply resistance at work. Resistance can come in the forms of either a sudden sense of being very tired, or sitting back and judging the process. Rather than fighting or judging the resistance, become present with it by returning to step 1, the **Diamond Self**. Simply, come into SHINE Time by breathing into the resistance wherever you may feel it in your body. If you feel tired, simply place your hands on your heart and belly and let the tiredness expand. Welcome it. Drop the fight. Remember, stillness is how you recharge your energy. Then, after a few minutes, continue your dialogue where you left off.

4. When in doubt, be Authentic! The key to this process is Authenticity. This is your sanctuary to be 100% real, which is your doorway to freedom. The truth shall set you free! So, in any given moment if you don't know how to move forward in any part of this process, express what is most authentic for you. For example, if you are dialoguing and suddenly get tired or you second-guess where to go from where you are, simply share your truth with the facet you are dialoguing with. *"I am tired. I have been tired my whole life and am so done trying to figure everything out. I just want to be at peace."* Then, pause and notice how you feel as you clearly speak what is true for you in this moment. Breathe into and allow what you feel as you continue the process.

5. Vulnerability is your strength. This is your chance to be vulnerable, given that you are in safe space and no one is around to fight you. Use this process to express from your heart, share your deepest needs, and voice your feelings, as you get comfortable with vulnerability. There is great power in seeing yourself beneath the façade that you may wear in your day-to-day life.

Materials:
1. **A private, uninterrupted space.** If you do not have privacy, you can work this process by writing in your journal, instead of doing the process through verbal expression.
2. **A candle and/or a flower(s).** Feel free to bring anything into the space that communicates a sense of sacredness.
3. **A journal and pen (or pencil).** After your **Diamond Process** session, you will want to write a few things down.
4. **Two pillows or two chairs** to alternate sitting on during the step that involves **Medicinal Dialogue**. I suggest two pillows if you are comfortable sitting on the floor. Breaking the routine and sitting on the ground brings a sense of adventure and openness. Doing so allows your senses to be fresh as you enter this new domain. Sitting on the floor is a simple gesture that has great power. If this is not comfortable, use two chairs facing one another.
5. **Your valuable Presence and an open heart.**

YOUR DIAMOND PROCESS SESSION:
Now to the full 7 Step Process. Let's get started...
  NOTE: If you need further guidance on any of the following steps, please revisit the corresponding chapter for each step in PART II.

STEP 1. THE DIAMOND SELF
Set up Sacred Space. Place two cushions, or two chairs, facing each other about two feet apart. One chair or pillow is for the *Diamond Self* and the other is for that which you are dialoguing with, which we will get into. Light a candle, place a flower in the environment, burn sage, say a prayer, or make any other gesture that communicates sacred space. (Your Space of Love is a great location for your *Diamond Process* Session.) Sit on one of the cushions. This is the seat of your *Diamond Self*.

Sit in the seat of the Diamond Self. Make yourself comfortable. Close your eyes, take a deep breath, and become present with your body. Breathe into your belly, relax wherever you can, and drop the agenda of trying to get somewhere completely. Bring all of your thoughts and energy back to yourself. Come home to your heart, five senses, and this very moment. Notice what is present in your body, emotionally, mentally, and physically. If your mind is busy and frantic, that is OK. Remember, being where you are and allowing what is, no matter how "messy," are how you empower the *Diamond Self*. Resistance creates suffering, so welcome whatever is present into this sacred space. Allow the *Diamond Self* to be awake to "what is" without trying to fix, eliminate, or change it. The key is to be open and curious, as if you are playing a challenging sport, or watching a movie rather than attempting to direct it. The *Diamond Self* is the witness, aware of everything and identified with nothing.

STEP 2. INTENTION SETTING
  Set your intention for this *Diamond Process* session. One of my favorites is, *"My intention is to heal at the deepest level available to me for my highest good and the highest good of all concerned."* This indicates that I am choosing to embody Wholeness, welcoming all of the orphaned facets back "home." So long as I am in this state of allowing, I can be present. When I am present, I am free. From Presence, everything works and falls into place. If you are struggling with health issues, you may set the intention to embody radiant health. These are just a couple of examples. This is an important step, as it is the "why" or purpose behind your *Diamond Process* session, which powerfully affects the direction, essence, and outcome (as discussed in chapter eight). Trust yourself and set your intention around what you choose to embody.

STEP 3. AWARENESS

Clarify the trigger that has knocked you off center and name how it makes you feel. What has created your upset and pulled you out of your ***Diamond Self***? How did it make you feel? The trigger may have been a person, an illness, "God," money, a home, or anything else that you feel charged around.

Simply complete this sentence:

I feel __(emotion)_ because ___(trigger)__.

(i.e., I feel sad because my boss did not like my performance on a project.)

Once you clarify this, say it out loud. If you are doing this by journal, simply write this under your intention statement.

Now, close your eyes and locate where in your physical body you feel the emotion. As you become aware of this trigger, is there a corresponding sensation in your body that feels uncomfortable? Whatever feeling you discover within yourself is a clue into a disowned "facet" of yourself that is asking to be accepted and integrated. For instance, it could be a facet of "regret" represented by a sense of heaviness in your heart and/or a tension in the throat. Maybe you have been trying to stuff this feeling down to avoid discomfort.

If there are several places where you feel tension, fatigue, or stuck energy, identify the area where it feels the strongest. If you don't feel anything in your body, that's okay too. As you learn to pay more attention to, and become present with, your body, the more your body awareness will expand. For now, knowing and feeling the emotion, or facet, that is present within you is enough to work your process.

Become deeply present with the feeling, free of thinking. Stay with your breath as you befriend and witness what you feel. If the sensation in your body and/or the emotion moves, simply follow and stay with it. Open up. Let it expand. This is your chance to do the opposite of what you have been doing, something that you likely learned, which is to cover, mask, or bury what you feel. Since emotions are energy in motion, they are meant to move. When we judge, resist or banish them, they become unnaturally lodged and hardened in the body. You may even consider giving an energetic thanks to this facet, or emotion, for showing itself to you by coming out of the shadow. Transformation is already happening by your willingness to simply allow this emotion to exist, and breathing into it, free of agenda.

Stay here in this state of openness, awareness, and acceptance for at least one minute. Often, especially once you are experienced with the **Diamond Process**, this will be enough to re-center you into your peaceful, authentic **Diamond Self**.

If you still feel unsettled, this provides an opportunity to work your process more deeply by dialoguing directly with the trigger, feeling in your body, or disowned facet of yourself.

STEP 4. MEDICINAL DIALOGUE

Choose the subject you feel emotionally charged towards and will be dialoguing with. Here are some examples:

i. A person you are upset with, or need to communicate something with (the trigger)
ii. Your Inner-Child
iii. An emotional or physical pain in your body
iv. A facet, or aspect, of yourself you are not proud of (i.e. "The Failure", Loneliness, etc)
v. The ego
vi. A figure, animal, or object that stood out in a dream, or in your waking life
vii. God, a deity, or spiritual figure

Bring your attention to the subject you are working with. Allow yourself to see and feel the essence of it in your mind's eye.

See the trigger or facet in detail. Visualize the color of their eyes, the texture of their skin, the tone of their hair, and feel their vibration. If you are dialoguing with a feeling, illness, or aspect of your personality, personify it into a "facet" (that is, if the aspect were a person or figure would it be...) by asking these questions:

- Is this facet masculine or feminine?
- Is this facet tall or short?
- What kind of hair, skin texture, body shape does this facet have?
- What is this facet wearing? What color is it's skin or clothes?

There is no way to get this wrong. Stay with the feeling rather than trying to figure it out. You may not see a person. Perhaps you simply see a shape or texture in your mind's eye. If so, what color and consistency is it? Alternatively, you may see nothing at all. If so, just stay with the sensations in your body.

Get a feel of its appearance and/or its essence.

In your mind's eye, call in the subject, or facet, to sit in the seat across from you. Obviously, you are not inviting the actual person to sit with you. This is simply about you sitting with the energy this person, figure, or facet embodies, similarly to your practice in chapter ten, *Using Medicinal Dialogue*. This is your chance to directly dialogue with them in honor of brave authentic expression, personal discovery, and freedom.

The power of transformation lives within you. You are the medicine. You are the way! The world out there, including the trigger, is simply reflecting back to you various facets of yourself that need your attention. As an example, whenever you feel strongly attracted to or repelled by someone, this is evidence that a disowned facet of yourself needs to be integrated with the rest of you. The trigger is the messenger poking and prodding at you, stirring up this disowned facet from within you so you can return to your *True Self* by embracing it. Communication, or *Medicinal Dialogue*, is a powerful way to look at your unconscious beliefs, commune with yourself, and reconnect with Love.

For example, by dialoguing with the trigger, you will discover how you think others are seeing you. In reality, this is simply a projection of what you have been judging about yourself. Whether or not "they" think what they think is irrelevant, and actually none of your business. Your business is YOU! Your use of *Medicinal Dialogue* will support you in clarifying the core belief that has been holding you back from living a fully expressed, love-filled life. Once you have this insight, you can upgrade your mindset and step more firmly into what your heart is choosing.

Remember, this isn't about getting rid of a feeling. This is about coming into Radical Authenticity and Self-Acceptance, while dropping the judgment, or rubble, that has kept you from loving yourself completely.

Personally, I recall feeling stuck and frozen months ago. I knew something was off because I felt so heavy and burdened, yet I had no idea what it was. As I started dialoguing with the heaviness, fury began to rise up from within me towards my beloved partner for no "logical" reason. Yet, the undeniable truth was I was feeling the anger and fury. If my mind tried to talk me out of it, or into figuring it out, I yet again would lose the realness, the transformational fire and freedom of letting the emotions express in safe, sacred space. This is a clever trick of the ego, designed to keep emotions locked up. So, be real with what you feel. This is the key to your freedom.

In this example as well as countless others, outside of my ego's comfort zone, once I let it all out, I grew free and unencumbered. I discovered in the dialogue that the feeling was from a much younger time in my life, which it usually is. It simply needed a current target to aim at (not literally, of course, but privately within my own sacred space) so that the emotion could be stimulated and set free. Unexpressed feelings and beliefs from the past will continue to project onto our current world until we speak our peace, see it for what it is, and move on. Often, upset with your husband or wife has nothing to do with them. It is simply a projection of unresolved hurt towards your mother or father. Once you get going with the dialogue, especially when you go straight to the source, or the earliest time you recall feeling something similar to what you currently feel, the pain is healed at the root. From there, every relationship transforms like a domino effect. The key is to stay open and honest with what arises in you moment to moment.

If you are not clear concerning what subject, or facet, to hold your dialogue with, consider speaking directly with your inner-child. This is an empowering opportunity to be with your younger self from the perspective of the loving, patient, authentic **Diamond Self**. Most of the pain we feel today is repressed emotion from childhood. Often what is needed most is to reach your hand back in time to hold the hand of your inner-child. In doing this, you get the opportunity to be the caring Presence that he or she so deeply needed during those vulnerable years. This simple act can become your own "homecoming" in which you re-parent your precious inner-child. As you do, listen deeply to become her (or his) hero. Remember, this is not about being perfect, but simply about including your inner-child in a conversation, being real, and allowing emotional expression as you grow together in communication and trust. I've seen hundreds of clients and students have radical breakthroughs by consistently and specifically working these **Medicinal Dialogue**s with their inner-child.

'Fess up and rise up with gusto. Once you have identified who or what you will dialogue with (i.e. your ex-husband, stomach pain, God, your inner-child, "The Screw Up" facet, the feeling of anger, etc.), you are ready to start your dialogue. This is your opportunity to give an unbridled voice to what you have been feeling.

SPEAK FROM THE SEAT OF THE DIAMOND SELF TO BEGIN THE MD, USING THE 5 ATTRIBUTES AS YOUR GUIDE:

Awareness - This is already something you are demonstrating by being with what you are feeling, free of judgment. The *Diamond Self* is already powering up here and now.

Authenticity - This is the most important attribute to embrace for *Medicinal Dialogue*. Whatever you are feeling right now is the doorway to awakening the *Diamond Self*. This is not about being politically correct. This is about radical transparency. Even though you may be feeling rage, anxiety, grief, or jealousy, all of which seem to be far removed from what you may perceive the *Diamond Self* to be... being real with what you feel is the key. In the beginning stages of using the *Diamond Process* you may feel like the *Diamond Self* is so far away. Over time, as you allow yourself to privately speak your truth, no matter how ugly it may seem, the unconditionally loving presence of the *Diamond Self* will begin to stir and strengthen from within. Be brave in your authenticity as you speak the "unspeakable."

Authenticity is especially valuable. When you are in the seat of the *Diamond Self*, as long as you are employing this attribute, you are blossoming into the *Diamond Self*.

Allowance - This shifts you from control to freedom. The degree to which one is suffering is equally proportionate to how tightly they grasp or resist life. Allowance provides you with your opportunity to "let go for dear life!"

There are only two guidelines here:
1. Be safe; do no harm to yourself or another, and...
2. If you are working with the energy of anger or rage, make sure that you turn it outward to an outside trigger or figure. The only person anger is not allowed to be expressed towards is yourself, including the innerchild.

Due to the fact that our culture views anger with shame, most of us have instead learned to repress it, which has created a sick society. In and of itself anger isn't bad, but is a natural response to injustice. When the energy of anger is not allowed expression towards whoever violated your boundaries (which is typically why anger arises), then it typically internalizes, eating away at oneself. This anger turned inward is a leading cause of society's depression. As my teacher, Leonard Jacobson has said, if everyone were to come into right relationship with anger, we would have a peaceful world. It's that simple! Allowing what you feel to be expressed safely and consciously, free of judgment, has the power to heal your life.

Acceptance - This is the power of embracing yourself and what you feel as you take full ownership of it. Rather than blaming the world "out there," which is synonymous with disempowering yourself, you accept that the feeling is within you and therefore it's also your responsibility. This is where you get to accept yourself radically and completely, which is the ultimate love story and path of empowerment.

Appreciation - This is the ability to be thankful for everything, including your greatest challenges, as opportunities for your soul's evolution. Can you appreciate that this trigger is bringing to the surface what has long been buried within you, and was silently limiting your life? Had the trigger not been there as a messenger, you would have continued walking around with the same pattern... playing small and harboring toxicity.

While you may feel far away from the enlightened *Diamond Self* that you picture in your mind during the dialogue, I assure you that in speaking bravely, rather than pretending, you are one giant step closer to your enlightenment. Shining light into the shadows with compassion, brightens your soul.

Initiate the dialogue from the seat of the Diamond Self. The easiest way to do this is to take a moment to call inward and feel the presence of who/what you are dialoguing with as if he/she/it is sitting right in front of you. Even if you are upset, consider honoring the energy you are dialoguing with from a place of appreciation. For example, *"Thank you for showing up, Mom. I have something I need to share with you."* This isn't about sugar coating with a false "thank you." This is about you knowing deep down within yourself that this dialogue is for your own healing and liberation.

Now, your Medicinal Dialogue begins... Take however long you need to say what you need to say as honestly and bravely as possible from the seat of the *Diamond Self*. This is about migrating from suppression to expression, in honor of freedom.

Then, when you feel complete, switch seats and respond from the other position, be it person, energy, or thing. Sit in it's seat, pause, and feel it's essence before responding from it's perspective.

Let the dialogue happen organically and let it rip. Explore letting the feeling express free range rather than trying to be contained or logical. Feelings are not rational. Often, they are raw and messy. Give yourself permission to express full-spectrum and color outside of the lines, so to speak. Drop any idea of the Diamond Self and simply speak as the raw, authentic you (given how you truly feel in this moment). Remember, authentic self-expression - free of judgment - helps you bloom into the Diamond Self.

Here is a short sample of what the Diamond Process session looks like, given what we have covered so far:

INTENTION STATEMENT: My intention is to heal at the deepest level available to me with ease and grace.

TRIGGER STATEMENT: I feel angry because my mom sent me a harsh email. She said that she is ashamed of me because I received financial support from my ex-boyfriend during a challenging time.

DIAMOND SELF: Thank you for coming forward for this dialogue, mom. I have something important to share with you.

MOM: What is it?

<> I feel very angry in response to the email you sent me and I need to talk about it honestly and clearly.

MOM: You're angry? I am the one who should be upset. I am ashamed of you! I never taught you to take handouts. I taught you to earn every penny, to work hard and prove your worth.

<> I really want to be calm right now, but I can't be. You are infuriating to me. I am a grown woman and you have no right to dump your judgments onto me. Strength, to me, is not about always being perfect and immune to vulnerability. At times, receiving support is just as noble as giving it.

MOM: Who taught you to live like "a failure"? This is disgusting. Get a job! I cannot believe this is my daughter.

<> I have a job and I am not just your daughter, mom. I am ME, a mature woman, with my own perspective and personal integrity. Just because I don't do things your way does not make me wrong.

(Pause. Silence. Breathing into the belly and feeling/allowing the fury. A ROAR comes out)

<> Respect me! Keep your opinion about me, and my life, to yourself. If you can't honor my request, then it's likely I'll be cutting off communication

with you. I am not making you wrong. I am just choosing to take care of me now. Your job is you. My job is me.

MOM: You are going to cut me out of your life for loving you? What has happened to you? The last thing I need is for you to cut me out of your life. I am your mother.

<> I understand and if you respect me, I am happy to be in communication with you.

MOM: It's hard to let go of my opinion, especially when I see you making such embarrassing mistakes.

<> That's it! I'm done. I have no more space for your demeaning opinion in my life. All I have ever wanted is for you to see me and accept me as I am. It's like going to the desert seeking water. I give up. We are done here!

(Pause. Turn within. Breathe into the emotion. Grief begins to rise up. Tears.) Continue switching seats and dialoguing until you feel complete. Then close the dialogue.

<> Mom, thank you. I now release you.

Envision the seat across from you cleared and close your eyes for a moment of Stillness.

4 Core Questions to pause with and ask yourself after your Medicinal Dialogue:

Once you fully express what you feel, you are ready to explore these 4 Core Questions. Remember, what you resist, persists. These core questions are designed to help you strengthen the ***Diamond Self*** by releasing resistance, dropping the fight and relaxing into the moment.

1. Am I willing to allow the trigger (i.e. mom) to exist without trying to change it/her?
2. What do I feel right now in my body and can I allow and embrace it?
3. What facet of me did this dialogue help me become aware of/discover (i.e. "The Failure")?
4. What does this revealed facet need from me?

For example, when tuning into the facet of "the failure," its need may be, *"I need you to accept and protect me."* Then, explore how you can tangibly do that. Ask, *"What is one way I can accept and protect you?"* It may respond with, "Can you let me express through free form writing once this week?" or *"Please put healthy boundaries up with mother. I need a healthy distance."*

If you worked with the Inner Child, a painful emotion, or a physical illness, it is equally important to explore what its deepest need from you is. You can apply the same inquiry to clarify its need from you.

Also, if you felt resistance to questions #1 and #2, simply notice and admit your resistance to allowing the trigger or the challenging feeling to exist. Be real with what you feel. This transparency alone creates awareness and momentum.

Find a way to supply the facet's need this week, if possible. If you know you will follow through, agree to take action in a way that is resonant and aligned with your heart. This may require negotiation with the facet, depending on what works for you. Be specific. Less is more. Only agree to what you can and will easily put into motion, or nothing at all. When your actions do not meet up to your words, you lose personal integrity. When your actions match your words, you build self-trust. Be true to your word.

Reminders and Considerations:

1) Within every trigger lives a treasure. Challenges are gifts in disguise that are designed to serve you in your evolution of returning to Wholeness. You can empower wholeness by coming into right relationship with this facet of yourself and taking action in a way that feels congruent with your North Star Intention.

2) The key is to drop any agenda and expectations. View this as an emotional-movement-meditation of sorts with nothing to fix. If your dialogue has many silent moments, great! This is simply an opportunity to discover and be present with what you feel within your dialogue as openly as possible. The emotions may change tones and take all kinds of unexpected directions. Sometimes they speak, sometimes they don't. Other times, you may be dialoguing with anger towards your girlfriend when you suddenly realize that you're really angry with your mother. With this realization, you can easily close the conversation with your girlfriend from the seat of the *Diamond Self* before calling in, and dialoguing with, your mother's energy.

3) Make the dialogue process your own- be authentic! Be as present as possible. If you look ahead and try to figure out where this is going, you'll get lost. If you do this, it's a perfect opportunity to come back to the breath, sit in SHINE Time, and then speak from there authentically. Just be present and honest in each moment and you'll remain on path.

4) This is an exploration, an opportunity to expand your awareness. This is your chance to see what has been going on in your unconscious. If you are using this process to get rid of what you are feeling, you are wasting your time. You will just exhaust yourself in a drama. On the other hand, if you use this to become present and see it as an opportunity for self-love, miracles can and will present themselves. Be ultra-aware of whether you are using this process to escape a feeling. If you are, 'fess up and rise up from the seat of the **Diamond Self**. *"I have to admit, I just realized I hate feeling x,y,z and I want to fix you."* You will likely feel liberated as soon as you catch yourself and maybe even laugh. Having this level of self-awareness and humility breeds a new sense of freedom and joy.

5) This process is designed to help you deepen in Presence and befriend all facets of yourself. Having a *Medicinal Dialogue* is one way of inviting up what you have been pushing down. This is a sacred sit, having tea, so to speak, to have a chat with and witness one particular facet of your self. As you welcome each facet in the moment, you venture farther into wellness. Rather than saying, *"No depression, go away,"* **Medicinal Dialogue** empowers you to say "Welcome, depression. I am here with you. I am not leaving." Notice the word "Welcome" and see it in this way, "You are Well. Come!" Wellness follows the inviting energy of welcome.

6) No matter how messy it may get, enjoy your MD. Remember that the lotus blooms out of the mud. No mud, no lotus! In the same way, the very muck that you've run from in the past is exactly what is needed for you to bloom into the energies of Presence, Love, and Acceptance.

STEP 5. OFFERINGS OF SELF-FORGIVENESS

Now that your dialogue is complete, you can clear the revealed belief systems from your mind as you make offerings of self-forgiveness to the part of you that innocently believed them.

Sitting in the seat of the Diamond Self, close your eyes and take a deep breath. Place one hand over your heart and one hand over your belly, connecting with yourself.

Move through the Obstacle Clearing Statement. This step is your golden key to freedom! Track and release any judgments

that came up during your MD, starting each sentence with ...
Anywhere I bought into the belief that (identify belief), I cancel, clear, and delete it and I forgive myself completely.

For example: Anywhere I bought into the belief that there is something wrong with me, I cancel, clear, and delete it and I forgive myself completely.
A few shortcut options for the OCS is ...

I forgive myself for judging myself as ...
I forgive myself for buying into the belief that ...
I forgive myself for buying into the misinterpretation of reality that ...

Keep going until you feel complete. You will know when you feel lighter. There is typically a core belief that is like the seed of the weed that was causing havoc. When you identify and offer yourself the gift of forgiveness, it will feel like you dropped a bag of bricks, or shall I say a ton of "rubble."

6. NO-THING-NESS

Once you feel complete with your offerings of self-forgiveness, you are ready to "make space for Grace." Now, I invite you to sit in the reality of having no story, no agenda, going nowhere, and doing nothing. This is your chance to let it all go...

1. See your story, and anything else you were holding onto, being dissolved. Imagine that you are sitting on the shore of a perfect, pristine beach and a wave gently washes over you and recedes back to the vast sea, carrying away your story, your thoughts, your agenda, and anything that just happened during this process.

2. Take a deep breath and sit in the spacious nothingness. With your eyes closed, be here and allow yourself to feel the freedom of this space. Your only job is to let go and breathe.

This is a sacred pause.

7. DECLARATIONS OF TRUTH

From the space of Stillness, verbally declare your destiny. Using the insight you gained from your self-forgiveness statements, now turn them around, *"The truth is...."*

For example:

The truth is I AM enough.

The truth is I AM designed to thrive.

The truth is I have been trying to fix myself my whole life and I am finally remembering how to radically accept myself.

The truth is I AM so grateful to be evolving in consciousness.

The truth is that even in the most challenging times there is a gift.

The truth is I AM love.

The truth is there is a way through every block.

The truth is I AM the way.

In your journal, write down one or all of your unique declaration statements. Circle the one that is the most powerful, representing the heartfelt truth you are claiming from this dialogue. Write it on an index card and post this card somewhere that you can see it daily.

Recognize that you have just further integrated a facet of yourself. By embracing what is, you have stepped more firmly into the *Diamond Self*.

This is you coming home. This is you using the substance and messiness of life to derive the message that your soul has been asking you to listen for. I celebrate you for having the courage to dive into this journey. You can use this process again and again, either written in your journal or spoken aloud in your Space of Love. Each time will be a unique experience, helping you deepen in Self-Inquiry, Self-Love, and expand into Wholeness.

BONUS TIP: What is one nugget of wisdom you have collected from this Diamond Process session?

Look for one insight you have gained and give thanks for it. Even if you still feel somewhat upset emotionally or physically, you may be aware that part of you is resisting and not accepting where you are. This awareness alone is something for which to be grateful. Self-Awareness is already creating transformation in your life, which is definitely something to appreciate.

Stay with your breath, trust this moment, and be gentle with yourself. I celebrate you for investing your time and energy in befriending yourself. This very process is evidence that you care for yourself deeply and are already embodying the *Diamond Self*.

Your Gem Power Declaration

"I AM bold enough to be whole."

Diamond Self Activation
Putting it into Practice...

1. THE 7-STEP DIAMOND PROCESS:
Use the full *Diamond Process* verbally in your Space of Love, or in your *Diamond Process* journal...

Step 1. Diamond Self: Call in sacred space and center yourself in Presence.

Step 2. Intention: Set your intention for your *Diamond Process* session.

Step 3. Awareness: Name the feeling and identify the trigger.

Step 4. Medicinal Dialogue: Give a voice to what you are feeling.

Step 5. Offerings of Self-Forgiveness: Identify limiting beliefs and forgive yourself for having bought into them.

Step 6. No-thing-ness: Pause and recalibrate.

Step 7. Declaration of Truth: Design your destiny by declaring the truth of your heart by turning around your mind's limiting beliefs, or rubble. Focus on appreciation.

DIAMOND SELF ACTIVATION (JOURNAL QUESTIONS)

*What core limiting belief did you discover during your Medicinal Dialogue?

*What Declaration of Truth are you now choosing to empower instead?

*What was your favorite part about this process?

"The Joy is in the doing."
Sadguru Shankaracharya

Lead Your Life With Love

You are a precious, powerful child of the Creator. Driven by your desires, your hands help shape our world in each and every moment. Do you understand the extent of the power within you? Do you know that you are infinite? Are you aware that your heart's desires are like invisible seeds planted within you that are meant to make love more visible in our world?

Even though the nature of modern society teaches us to believe that authority lies in the hands of others, in reality, you are the author of your life story. The only time that your life was in the hands of others was during your childhood. It was then when you relied on your parents or primary care givers, teachers, and even world leaders, to direct your life. Early on, in one way or another we all learned to dim our connection to the Source of all power within us, innocently trading the Infinite for the finite. In doing so, we also innocently forgot our native origins as divine sparks and joyful co-creators.

Even in our education system, rather than nurture our innate desire to discover and explore, we're fed information from the outside to memorize.

Rather than digging deep into our *Inner Purpose*, instead we learn to trade the music of our hearts for the noise of the world. For the most part we are trained to become "followers of fear" rather than Leaders of Love; to be docile rather than daring. Even still, regardless of all past conditioning, today, you have the power to courageously lead for and from your heart. You are a creation of love, designed to love boldly and bravely, which is what these heartfelt words are encouraging you to remember.

YOUR OUTER PURPOSE REQUIRES MAINTAINING YOUR VIBRATION

As we discussed in Part I of this book, your unchanging *Inner Purpose* is to be present, which serves as a foundation for your ever-evolving life. On the other hand your outer purpose changes over time as your interests, circumstances, and desires evolve. Whatever you are living right now in your life is actually part of the evolution of your outer purpose. Yet regardless of how desirable or undesirable your current circumstances are, your sacred mission is to maintain your vibration. For example, if you are an accountant who's bored out of his or her mind, and all the while wishing you could pursue a career as an artist, your task is to remain in a state of appreciation for what you have now, while patiently moving in the direction of your artistry.

Leading your life with love has a lot to do with accepting yourself where you are as you cultivate who you are inspired to be. It also requires that you love yourself so much that you give yourself permission to put yourself and your vibration first because your "job" is YOU. Your purpose is YOU. Your service to the world is becoming who you are meant to be... the best version of YOU possible! **What you do** is far less important than how you do it. Are you moving with stress and overwhelm, or are you present, calm, and kind? If you are feeling stressed or overwhelmed, are you beating yourself up for it or are you loving and accepting yourself anyway?

Personally, my journey into leading with love started in 2004 when I began prioritizing what my heart desired to create. I left Corporate America, started my Masters in Spiritual Psychology, and actively created something new for myself. In doing so I started to open up to the power that is within me again as I realized that I have a choice in how I design my life. I also began to trust that the Universe has got my back, which took a *huge* leap of faith. The dreamer in me started to awaken as I rekindled the joy of using my imagination to weave together a more authentic and inspiring life. I went from feeling stuck to being alive. Yet, as you know from my story in chapter one, even in creating a beautiful new life for myself, lasting peace continued to elude me.

I began this whole outer adventure only to discover I'd completely neglected my *Inner Purpose*, devotion to the *Present Moment*, and loyalty to the *Diamond Self*. In beginning my outer adventure I failed to realize that one's outer purpose is built upon the foundation of *Inner Purpose*. Without a solid foundation, even a palace will shake and eventually collapse against life's strong and inevitable winds.

Even though this chapter is devoted to inspiring you around your outer purpose, please remember that being *Present* as often as possible is primary, for when you are connected to the *Present Moment*, peace, love, and joy flow from within you into all that you do. Whether you wake up on the wrong side of the bed one day, or things go your way on another, your *Inner Purpose* will elegantly and effortlessly carry you without fail, allowing you to feel centered, whole, and on purpose through any experience that life presents to you.

LIFE IS A LIVING, BREATHING, SPARKLING MIRACLE

In order to illustrate how powerful you truly are, I am going to share a miracle that I experienced over the last few months as I was writing this book. While this is normally something that I would keep quiet and close to my heart, I feel a nudge from within to share this with you, knowing that this sacred occurrence is also for you.

Several times along my spiritual journey, I have touched both bliss and indescribable insight into the miracle of life. We have all had peak experiences where the hidden beauty and perfection of life becomes apparent. These sacred moments are like touchstones that remind us to keep moving forward as we trust that there is more to life than meets the eye.

For me, nearly every time that deeper truth has been revealed, it did so while I was perfectly still, either reclined on the couch reading a high-vibrational book, sitting in nature enjoying SHINE Time, or on retreat feeling deeply relaxed. Within these mysterious occurrences what I experienced was a deep cellular calm (followed by bliss), which was simultaneously blessing me with a miracle.

In these unpredictable moments of all-encompassing silence, a secret of life is revealed to me. While breathing into my body and softening my gaze on a single object in the room, a white, sparkling mist rushes into my field of vision that fades the boundaries of each object in my view as it heightens a sense of **aliveness** within and around me. To put it simply, all of the content in the room that is in my field of vision morphs into one sea of pure, captivating light.

During my most recent experience with what can only be described as Grace, I was sitting at the dining room table after eating breakfast. I picked up a book, "Satsang with Baba" by Muktananda, that my beloved Jason had left on the table. After reading a few paragraphs, I set it down to digest both my breakfast and Muktananda's words. Sitting in perfect stillness, I felt so grateful and present.

On that particular morning, I had been looking out the window at the trees being swayed by the gentle breeze, the beauty of the bold surrounding mountains, and the colorful birds in flight before bringing my gaze down to the table, the book, and my empty plate. My mind was absolutely silent as I was present with the ordinary, taking in what was right in front of me. Within a few minutes of this stillness, everything began to spontaneously dissolve into this mysterious Light. My environment suddenly seemed to be dreamlike and surreal. When I looked at my hands, they too were light. From this perspective it appeared as though I could put my hand through the table, being that both were simply sparkling space. Moments before what had appeared to me to be solid matter now appeared to be this dynamic, glittery light that was seemingly intangible from this heightened level of **Consciousness**.

To those of you who have never had such an experience, I imagine this sounds like a science fiction novel, or perhaps the result of some psychedelic drug experience. Yet, with the exception of a few glasses of wine a year, I am a purist and use no form of drugs or alcohol whatsoever. These experiences are simply the result of deep, precious moments of **Awakened Presence**, which given the proper conditions is accessible to each and every one of us.

In that moment as I floated in a sea of consciousness, I realized that from a greater reality, everything in form, including my physical body, is simply light vibrating at a slower frequency. I began to have a sense of what Einstein meant in saying that, "Reality is merely an illusion, albeit a very persistent one." You know the light that shines through images as it's projected onto a movie screen? It was as if the strip of images was pulled away and I could see the source that illuminated them all. Sparkling light... Sparkling Consciousness... Truth!

One part of me was in awe and wanted to hold on to the experience. (Just so you know, this never works.) Yet another part of me wanted it to end due to the terror I felt well up inside me as I witnessed my own body-identity dissolving into this One Light. This particular experience was stronger than any I'd had in the past as it felt as though I, Veronica, was about to disappear. Yet whether out of a hunger to know God, or perhaps out of an unquenchable thirst for adventure, I stayed with it. In doing so, what I realized was that I was seeing my True Self... the **Diamond Self**... this sparkling formless **Presence**, that's at the center of everything and everyone.

The more I stayed present, the more awe I felt. On a deeper level, I realized that life is an unsolvable Mystery and rather than trying to control it, my purpose is to invoke and surrender to it. Just next to the book there was also a dollar bill, which Jason had been using as a bookmark. What I discovered as I gazed at this green, rectangular slip of paper was that this dollar bill, in essence, is also made of the same source of light as the book, my hand, and everything else. Differentiation and value is simply the byproduct of belief and perspective, which varies between each of us depending on our conditioning. One person can see money and light up while another feels a pit in their stomach at the sight of a stack of cash... same money, different perspective.

To say this in another way, what I could see from this illuminated perspective is that **everything** is neutral and part of the same Source. The positive or negative charge that we perceive is only due to the value and meaning that each of us ascribes to anything. Everything depends on how you see it and use it. Do you see money as the root of all evil or neutrally as a convenient way of exchanging goods and services? Do you judge a meditation cushion as better than a couch cushion? Is one person more lovable than another because they're more kind to you than someone else?

This experience taught me that in each moment, we have the power to ask a valuable question...

In this moment, am I being a follower of fear or a Leader of Love? In other words, are you in judgment or Radical Acceptance, criticism or Compassion, worry or childlike Wonder? Are you a victim of circumstance or a Co-Creator of Infinite Possibilities? Are you lost in separation or invoking Oneness? In each moment, you have a choice.

Seeing this reality with my own eyes, and not just reading about it in a book, powerfully transformed something in me. The first few times this happened, I didn't understand the experience. I simply felt bliss and awe. Yet this time it opened my mind to the true power of perspective. With this experience I gained a visceral understanding that my beliefs literally contribute to "forming" my reality. In seeing life as One Light, and remembering that we as people are also this light, it became clear that each of us are in-form-ing and influencing the shape of our lives with each thought, spoken word, and action. With this revelation, imagine that the depth of your love determines whether you add to the problems in the world or serve as their solution. When your focus is negative and you are complaining about life, you create more strife. Yet when your focus is positive and you are celebrating life, you nurture the Miracle.

As human beings, we cannot separate ourselves from God, Source, or whatever you want to call the Great Mystery. We are **one with** God. Like countless puzzle pieces making up this miraculous dream called Life, each piece is necessary and divine. No matter how pretty or ugly you perceive your life to be in this moment, **you are necessary and divine**. You cannot escape your native divinity. You are the **One** you have been waiting for. You are the Light. You are the Way!

LIFE IS A BEAUTIFUL, MYSTERIOUS SPORT

That very morning I realized that I had been putting my meditation cushion in the "good" pile, and money in the "bad" pile. My ego had become spiritualized, somehow taking life and her magnificent Mystery and cutting it up into fragments of right and wrong, deciding I know... the answers!

The truth is, as the blessed Sadguru Shankaracharya wisely invites his devotees to contemplate, *"Are you part of the problem, or are you part of the solution?"* I could be sitting on a meditation cushion, lost in my mind, thinking about how terrible life is, or I could be holding a hundred dollar bill in my hand with deep gratitude in my heart for the food it will buy me and my family. Which act is more "spiritual"? It's never the object of our attention, but rather how we relate to it.

On that mystical morning my perspective took a quantum leap. Ironically, it's not that I felt like I knew more. I actually felt that I knew less, which somehow softened my heart. I took a good look at my relationship with money and the material world, as well as many other things in my life. I explored everything in form as born from the same Source. I could feel this light of the **Diamond Self** mysteriously shining at the heart of everything, including you and me.

The Yogis call life a "Leela," which is literally translated into "a sport" in Sanskrit. This "sport" is divinely designed to be fun and challenging as we learn how to play, rain or shine, with Love while overcoming fear. If the Yogis are on to something and life really is one, beautiful, mysterious sport, how would you "play" differently? Would you frustratingly kick and scream, or exuberantly dance and sing? Would you isolate or collaborate? How **present** would you be through each and ever step?

In your everyday life, you can either see challenges as a punishment, or you can use triggers to awaken the treasure within. You can use money wisely as you purchase what you value, need, and love (knowing that God is your Source), or you can continue living in judgment, lack, and fear. You can either blame and battle against people who rub you the wrong way, or you can simply bless them, knowing that they are teachers in disguise, refining you into a more masterful "player" and Leader of Love.

You have the power every single day to look in the mirror, cherish what you see, and genuinely whisper, *"I love you as you are, sweet one. You're doing great!"* You are a child of God. You have the unshakable power within to lead your life with love and contribute to the creation of a healthy, beautiful, inspiring world. Step by step, thought after thought, breath upon breath, it is up to you.

That day, as I continued to sit in the seat of the **Diamond Self**, I realized how little I know, how mysterious our universe is, and how grateful I am that life is so much grander than I could ever conceive with my amazing little mind. I could also see that the miracle in everything is here now and not in some distant future. The miracle is right under your nose, beneath your feet, and literally within you. You are the miracle. How you relate to this moment defines how you will live in an ideal future. When you relax and court Grace wherever you are in the **Present Moment**, your destiny can naturally bloom in accordance with your full potential... and the best part is, in enjoying the journey, you are empowering the true destination- the world of Now!

THE POWER OF IMAGINATION

Life is infinite as are you, my friend. The very dreams that pulse through your pure heart are here to evolve and awaken this world. Every single human being has been given the power to imagine something that, as of yet, doesn't even exist. Whatever you desire from the heart has tremendous evolutionary power, especially when it fuels and informs your imagination. Everything in our world, including the very computer I am writing on right now, was first created through somebody's desire to experience something better than what was once available. When the desire is strong enough, and the practice of imagining a new reality sets in, infinite possibilities can be made manifest.

The evolution of life depends on our desires, imaginations, and inspired actions. Everything in nature is designed to activate desire. Berries are designed in bright colors to draw our attention and stimulate our hunger to eat them, inevitably spreading their seeds. Male hummingbirds are adorned with beautiful designs and colors to lure the female. Women's bodies are designed to be fit and voluptuous during fertile years to stimulate a man's arousal, therefore leading to an abundant growth in population. Desire is part of the divine design. Within the human mind, desire first leads to imagination and from there to expansion.

As Einstein so beautifully said, *"Imagination is more important than knowledge. It is the preview of life's coming attractions."* To say that the mind is a hindrance to us is like saying that a magic wand is a hindrance to a magician. When we become more present and remember that the mind does not use us, but we use the mind, a whole new destiny awakens and it is happening Now. This is the evolution of consciousness and creation working together for the greater good.

USE YOUR IMAGINATION TO CREATE (NOT ESCAPE) YOUR REALITY

The **Present Moment** is your eternal friend in which a great love affair with life sparkles open when you unconditionally place it first in your life. The key to leading your life with love is simple: Enjoy your **present moment** so much, through the deep practice of self-love and radical acceptance, that imagining and dreaming are simply a means for you to create, rather than being a source of your escape. Realize that your imagination is a resource of massive power that lies in wait within you. This power can either be used to exclusively feed your "me, me, me story," or it can be used to serve the Whole (including you) as you lead with Love.

We live in a world of contrast where we are constantly choosing what we like from what we don't like. In the clarity we gain from life experience, we start to dream up what we desire, creating a beautiful map of what destiny looks like. We are the only species on Earth that has the power of imagination.

Throughout this book, I have written a lot about migrating from the thinking mind into **Presence** by inviting you to bring the practice of SHINE Time into your daily life. If you don't feel more established in the **Present Moment**, I invite you to prioritize this **Inner Purpose** first and foremost before using your imagination to lead your life with love. If being Present is difficult for you, then you may consider using the full Diamond Process to free repressed emotions that may be blocking your ability to relax. If you leap into your imagination from a place of disempowerment or anxiety by running from pain, then you will likely create a limited possibility for yourself. Again, the key is to find your unique way into establishing your consciousness in the **Present Moment**, first and foremost.

This isn't about being a perfect Buddha who is present all the time, but just about having some connection to the flower on your desk, the pen in your hand, or the sensation of your heart beating in this moment. This is simply about opening up to what is in front of you in each moment, dropping resistance, and feeling more at home in the seat of the **Diamond Self** each and every day. Before chasing another dream that will likely exhaust you, fill your cup by celebrating what you already have now. Once you feel confident and more loyal to the **Present Moment**, you are ripe and ready to use the power of imagination from your heart. Rather than attaching yourself to a desired outcome, simply enjoy imagining for the sake of play, creating a paradise in your mind, and noticing if and how it shows up in your day-to-day life. The key is to have fun as you openly explore the power of your imagination as one of many tools for building your life with Love.

The easiest way to know if you are using your imagination out of fear or Love depends on whether or not you feel enthusiastic about it. The word enthusiasm comes from the Greek word, "enthusiasmus," which means "divine inspiration." It is this form of inspiration that stems from your heart and spirit. Anytime you think you "should" do something, or criticize yourself in any way, this is simply feedback that you are navigating off course. If you imagine having the perfect body because you are ashamed of your thighs or belly fat, this only exacerbates self-rejection and fear. When you lead your life out of guilt, shame, fear, or worry, you're hushing the "Power of Self-Love" and thus veering away from your authentic path. Clear signs that you are leading your life with fear are feelings of: depletion, competition, overwhelm, a sense of being overpowered by negative people and draining influences, waking up dreading your day, feeling lost, critical, drowning in survival mode, or feeling alone and depressed.

However, when you follow your enthusiasm in the same way that a child dances in the rain (and thus making the best of any given circumstance), even when any of these negative feelings arise, you'll recognize them as stemming from fear and lovingly let them go. For example, if you feel overwhelmed, you may choose to take a few things off of your plate and slow down even when it seems impossible for you to do so. When enthusiasm is the engine of your life, you become a bold expression of love, starting with Self-Love.

YOUR AUTHENTIC DREAMS ARE GUIDING YOU TOWARDS YOUR UNIQUE DESTINY!

If you have been talked out of what you truly love (and leaving your dreams behind), consider this chapter to be your **wake up** call. You are designed to serve our world by being present in all ways, including being present to yourself and your heartfelt dreams. Remember that your authentic dreams are clues guiding you like stars in the night towards your unique destiny.

Just like anything else, though, actualizing your unique potential requires planting yourself in healthy conditions, or what I refer to as your **Genius Habitat**. You know you are there when you gain energy from your environment and the activities in which you participate. In the same way that a pianist goes straight to the piano when he is stressed, or a basketball player shoots hoops to blow off steam and raise her frequency, what you are most inspired by has the power to regenerate you. What inspires you has the power to serve and inspire others as well.

JUST ONE YES STEP (J.O.Y.S.)

If you feel drained and completely departed from your **Genius Habitat**, taking "Just One Yes Step" (J.O.Y.S.) is how you can create momentum toward leading your life with love. The adventure of a lifetime begins with a single step and the fact that you are reading this book indicates that you have already taken a soul-centered leap.

Taking just one yes step emphasizes the power of patience and trusting that slow, relaxed, and steady action in the direction of what feels good to your heart really does win the race. One of the mistakes I often see people make is setting up large, rapid, insurmountable goals only to fall in disappointment when they do not reach their desired outcome. Sadly enough, this approach also hinders Self-Trust. However when you set one, manageable, heart-centered goal at a time, and patiently follow through with it, this approach will create a solid sense of Self-Trust within you.

Moving with this sort of patience and inner-loyalty not only sets you up for "true success," it also calms the ego, as the ego does not like change. Therefore, it is equally important to take enthusiastic steps while honoring the ego by making sure each of them is easily "digestible." When you come into this type of respect and harmony with all dimensions and facets of yourself, including the ego, revealing the **diamond** that you are unfolds in a gradual, peaceful, and joyful manner.

Celebration of who you are in this moment, and appreciation for the ground you are now walking upon, no matter how muddy it may seem to be, will set you free onto the path of Leading Your Life with Love. As you do less with **presence** and celebration rather than doing more with stress and expectation, you are stepping into true success. Remember, this moment is the destination. If you can notice and appreciate one sprout of life cracking through a city street on your walk to a meeting and smile, you are transforming your mindset and embracing the "yesness" of life! This is what I consider "JOYS" (Just One Yes Step). This is but one way of creating super-fertile inner conditions and maintaining a high vibration. Rather than being sucked into the mind, you can marry the **present moment** instead, activating your everlasting "in-love glow."

A few more examples of taking Just One Yes Step may be:
- Drink one organic green juice or eat one salad a day
- Go to bed early, ensuring you get eight hours of sleep
- Take a 20-minute walk around your neighborhood
- Send a heartfelt cover letter and your resume to a business that inspires you
- Meditate under a tree for 20 minutes
- Practice SHINE Time as you eat lunch, being mindful with each bite
- Buy one article of clothing that expresses who you are as a leader of Love
- Book a massage
- Hire a housekeeper
- Start a gratitude journal
- Drink eight glasses of water a day
- Post self-love notes all over your home and office
- Hire a life coach
- Take a yoga class
- Volunteer with an organization you cherish

- Get your hands in the soil and plant a native tree
- Read one chapter in a high-vibrational book
- Detox from mainstream news
- Enjoy a tech-free day
- Take a Forgiveness Stay-cation
- Start and end your day with 3 statements of gratitude
- Go on a date with your inner-child. Do something fun!

FOUR CORE HUMAN NEEDS TO SUPPORT YOUR OUTER PURPOSE

As humans we have four basic needs that need to be met in order to lead a life of love:
1. To feel safe and secure
2. To love and be loved
3. To feel like you belong
4. To make a beneficial contribution

In the next few paragraphs, we will look at how you can, feel safe, loved, make a meaningful contribution, and feel a sense of belonging within a resonant community.

1. Security is an Inside Job - Embodying *Presence* and Radical Self-Acceptance is the ultimate form of security. Being identified with the *Diamond Self* rather than your temporary body, passing emotions, and fleeting thoughts is the path of confidence and unshakable security. True security is a willingness to remember that you are in the world, but not of it. You are infinite in your ability to love and accept every facet of yourself. You are a spiritual being having this human experience. Security is an inside job that is accomplished by loving and accepting your humanness unconditionally while remembering that who you truly are is the Sparkling Awareness behind every word, thought, sensation, and action within your life's story.

2. You are already a Leader of Love - You were born to be a leader of love. This is crystal clear when you observe how children live before they learn how not to live. Early on, they are so good at giving and receiving love. They are stellar at imagining and creating their reality. They are experts at authentic expression and asking for what they need. They are fantastic at being vulnerable, allowing what they are feeling to really be there. Their appreciation for the wonder and magic of life is natural. They may not yet have words for "thank you," but their eyes and smiles roar with appreciation.

You, too, were born with these qualities and since you have attracted this book into your hands, it is clear that you are also choosing to live as a heart-centered leader. A Leader of Love sees, thinks, speaks, listens, and acts purely, consciously, and authentically. Leading with Love does not exclude fear; it actually entails acknowledging it and moving onward with **presence**, trust, and truth anyway. When you choose to lead your life with love, you are aware that you have a choice in how you move forward in life. You can feel energized every day, set healthy boundaries, and focus on sharing yourself symbiotically with those you genuinely resonate with. You can hold yourself with the same patience and care you would demonstrate with a small child.

In this state of being you embrace yourself, take a good look at what you have been believing about life, and lovingly close old deals and contracts with those who no longer serve you. This is an ongoing, life-long process that becomes natural again over time. Now in league with Spirit you become the co-author of your life and co-designer of your destiny, as you choose what wholeheartedly lights you up while surrendering to the highest unfolding. Once and for all, you know that living a life of love is your birthright. Having dropped the belief that any authority lies outside of you, you become empowered and intentional as you celebrate life, trusting your journey's wonderful, mysterious unfolding step by step.

QUESTIONS OF SELF-INQUIRY TO SUPPORT YOU AS A LEADER OF LOVE

- What matters most to my heart?
- What are the non-negotiables in my life that support my wellbeing?
- Where in my life are things asking for my attention?
- What are my regular complaints in life truly about?
- Where am I caught in victim mentality?
- Where I am withholding my truth? Why?
- Where am I resisting life's challenges?
- How can I let go?
- How is my day-to-day language limiting or empowering me?
- Am I keeping my word and promises to myself?
- What incomplete cycles of action are asking for completion

in my life?
- Where do I need to stretch myself in order to lead my life with Love?
- What is the most empowering question I can ask myself right now?

3. Your Ability to Fully Be Yourself With Others Creates Genuine Belonging - Leading your life with love requires a strong commitment to being authentic with others. Having the courage to be witnessed cultivates a sort of bravery that frees you into living your truth and making choices from your heart, regardless of the opinions of others. When you can be open, vulnerable and intimate with at least one other loving, resonant person, a sense of belonging flowers within your heart, which empowers love and a sense of true family.

Empowering this sense of belonging is also supported by exercising discernment. Creating a sense of belonging requires a willingness to recognize that you may be better off loving some people from a distance, while courageously sharing with others closely and transparently. Having a sense of genuine belonging does not mean that you have to be fully exposed with everyone you encounter. All that is needed is at least one friend, mentor, or member of your "family" with whom you are willing to authentically share yourself.

4. Your Vibration is Your Contribution to the World - Your Life is Your Message. Being present in the moment and playfully expressing yourself is a powerful way to give back to our world. When you are calm and loyal to your soul, it is easy to give because you are not sourcing from an outward recognition, but by recognizing that you are the *one* you have been waiting for. When you are devoted to mastering your first core need, by creating an inner-sense of safety and security, your life naturally becomes a beneficial contribution. Rather than seeking outward approval, you naturally enjoy giving back, as you feed love and inspiration into the world through your example.

In addition, outer purpose typically has a direct correlation with your deepest wounds. The very wounds that you thought you needed to bury are the ones that not only have the potency to awaken the *Diamond Self*, but they also contain the clues concerning the cargo that you are here to deliver. The very things you wrestle with and overcome hold the very gems you are here to contribute to the world. I have seen this time and time again with clients: the shyest woman in her family becomes a Self-Expression Coach, or the man who suffers from gastritis and terrible anxiety becomes a guide on Mindful Eating. The stars do not determine your destiny. YOU DO! The stars, fate, and the fixed facts that revolve around the time and place of your birth give rise to the block of marble you get to work with. You can either leave it, believing you are stuck behind a thick boulder, or you can feel deeply, get in touch with what you desire from the depth of your heart, and then carve and carve and carve as you put your life's outer purpose into action, which always starts with your *Inner Purpose*.

So the question is, what are you creating? What wound were you given to crack you open enough to find your own unique path back to Love? What mess are you here to bless with a message of divine inspiration that's designed to satiate a hunger that only you can fill? What is your piece of this mysterious puzzle of life? How present, loving and conscious are you willing to be, knowing that your vibration is your real contribution to the world?

AWAKENING THE TREASURE WITHIN

Personally, even though I saw my mother's illness as a curse, something I wished I could erase from my story and my family's reality for decades, I now see it as the greatest treasure in disguise. By witnessing what terrified me within my mother, I learned to run. Yet in running away from her, and away from my own wildness, I finally exhausted myself. Once that happened, I fell hard. For me, collapsing was, as it often is, the first step to rising up from the ashes and allowing the *Diamond Self* to finally shine through.

Had I had the perfect, balanced mother, I never would have been ignited into seeking my true path and what it means to be a healthy, empowered expression of the divine feminine. Without learning to hush my authentic voice, I never would have experienced the joy of liberating the roar that once only whispered, experiencing deep healing, and adventuring through radical transformation. I never would have been bruised enough to head for the soft redwoods, where I ultimately birthed this very book and process; one that is supporting countless people around the world in discovering who they truly are.

Within your wounds, live your greatest blessings. All of those years of denying I was my mother's daughter, living in silent resentment for her "ruining" my life, and maybe even blaming myself for her pain, I was preparing to live my outer purpose without even knowing it. Fighting against my own pain with polish was all part of my soul's plan. There are no mistakes. Once I reached enough pain, fought hard enough and hid long enough, I began to realize that I am not only my mother's daughter, but I am now proud to be so. Women like my mother are not here to be tamed or understood... and neither am I.

Instead we are here to set our fires free so that diamonds can be born. We are here to remind the world that perfect is not the image of model looks, high-paying jobs, or idyllic family dynamics. Perfect is simply a state of being and it is especially in the face of our flaws that we get to come to this realization of radical self-acceptance. It is deep at the heart of this messy, marvelous thing that we call being human, that an unbreakable, divine love can be found inside which shines through anything.

If you are lucky (yes, lucky), you'll encounter enough friction, be exposed to enough heat, and face just enough pain to finally surrender, embrace yourself completely, and let the diamond within you awaken and rise. Picking up a book like this one is a sure sign that you are welcoming such a miracle into your life. The leader of love within you is calling and you are listening, evolving our humanity to the next level through your courage, devotion to Presence, and willingness to let your heart sing like no one is listening.

My heart sings to remind you that you are valuable without having to lift a finger. Your vibration and state of being is your contribution to our world. Your sensitivity can actually be your strength and... you, dear one, are not designed to be like everybody else. You were born to be wholly, freely, and authentically you. You were created to naturally *shine* in the way that only you uniquely can. You have never happened before and will never come again through all eternity. This is it. Right now. This body. This breath. This moment. Just this.

You *are* the treasure.

Your Gem Power Declaration

I AM A LEADER OF LOVE.

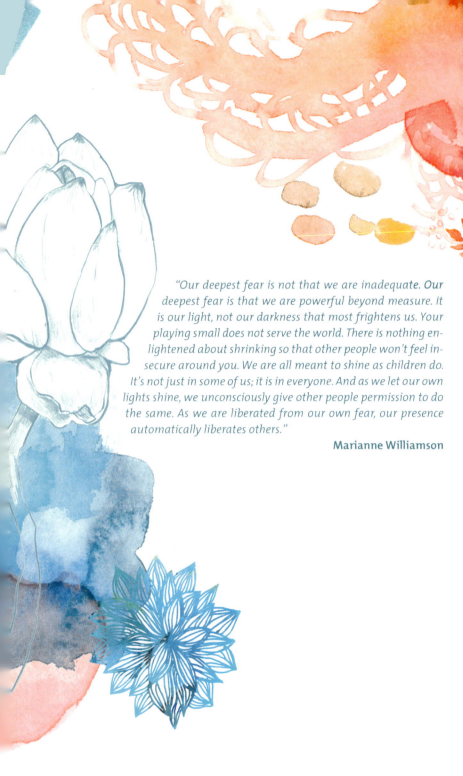

"Our deepest fear is not that we are inadequate. Our deepest fear is that we are powerful beyond measure. It is our light, not our darkness that most frightens us. Your playing small does not serve the world. There is nothing enlightened about shrinking so that other people won't feel insecure around you. We are all meant to shine as children do. It's not just in some of us; it is in everyone. And as we let our own lights shine, we unconsciously give other people permission to do the same. As we are liberated from our own fear, our presence automatically liberates others."

Marianne Williamson

To expand your Diamond Process experience, I invite you to join the global community at **VeronicaKrestow.com** to receive the *Treasure Tuesdays* video series and other free exclusive resources.

ACKNOWLEDGMENTS

I WOULD LIKE TO THANK the growing number of women and men around the world who are firmly devoted to spiritual growth and leading with Love. Your self-transformation is a bold contribution to our human family.

Thank you to my beloved, Jason, for being an unshakable pillar of Presence, wisdom, humor, and love in my life. One of the greatest privileges I get to enjoy daily is adventuring the world (inner and outer) with you. I love thee and am deeply blessed to share my life with you.

Thank you to Leonard Jacobson for introducing me to the world of the Present Moment. Your teachings have not only transformed my life over the last decade, but have radically influenced this book. There are no words to capture my gratitude for you and your guidance into Freedom and Oneness.

R.R. Lowinger, thank you for being a "facilitator of dreams," for having helped me to remember all those years ago that I can write, and more than anything for loving and believing in me during a time when I had lost hope.

Thank you to my soul friends and family for all of your encouragement, support, and celebration around creating this book. Kim, Jonathan, Jeanne, Shirly, Astrid, Caroline, Steven, Dror, Rebekah, Noushin, to name a few. Your enthusiasm around my writing has kept me keepin' on again and again.

A special thank you to my father, Victor, for reminding me that I wrote my first book at six years old and have not stopped writing since. Thank you for serving as a "lighthouse" in my life and my work.

A heartfelt thank you to Alena Guest and Steve Siler for so dearly holding sacred space for me during my time in the redwoods... and beyond. Your wise guidance and example of healthy home and partnership has helped me find a better way to live, love, and lead today.

To the beloved Drs. Ron and Mary Hulnick for teaching me to unlearn who I am not, exposing me to Gestalt therapy as well as many other Spiritual Psychology techniques, and helping me build a strong, self-honoring foundation that continues to support me, my growth, and soul-centered service.

A very special "thank you" to each and every client, Love-inar participant, and Diamond Retreat Sister for trusting me and the Diamond Process with your most honest and vulnerable moments. You, too, have been my teachers, reflecting priceless feedback for fine-tuning this transformational work and who I Am as an authentic leader of Love.

Thank you to Marianne Williamson for your divine teachings, feminine leadership and loving heart. At a time when everything was falling apart in my life, I had the rare privilege of meeting you. Your words, which I will never forget, served like a light at the end of the tunnel, showing me that a seemingly small act of kindness can be the seed of a great, new beginning, which is exactly what your words were for me.

Thank you to my YouTube family for giving me a safe space to share my heart so honestly all of these years. Your love, kindness, and appreciation have taught me that it is safe to be raw and transparent while sharing my gifts in the world.

With tremendous gratitude to my amazing team: Marisa Nakhi for your stellar coaching, affirmative prayers, and publishing guidance; Natalie Neumann for your brilliant illustrations, branding, and taking the vision of this book to another level of beauty; and Jim Rogers, my amazing editor. You are gifted with (and beyond) words! Without each of you and your stellar talent, this book would have remained an ever-changing file on my computer in a never-ending refinement process. Thank you for helping me to let go and birth this "book baby" with ease.

... and a very special "thank you" to Sadhana Ashram and the blessed and beloved Sadguru Shankaracharya. Thank you for your Grace, your teachings of Truth, and for helping me surrender and remember that I am a "Big Tree." Jai Ma, Guruji!

Veronica Krestow is a Spiritual Mentor and Transformational Coach whose message of radical self-acceptance and love has attracted thousands of people worldwide to her courses, retreats, and popular Youtube channel which has received well over half a million views. Veronica grew up in Miami Beach where the materially focused culture left little room for authenticity and spiritual discovery. At 32-years old, she was living a thriving life in Los Angeles and on the verge of marriage with a wonderful man when a painful realization took place in her heart prompting her to leave everything behind and discover her true self.

Today, having received a Masters in Spiritual Psychology, she leads an acclaimed transformational coaching business worldwide helping clients to break through suffering and step into inspiring freedom, purpose, and true power. With her refreshing perspective on using challenges to awaken who you truly are, or what she calls "The Diamond Self," she is accomplishing her soul's mission to help everyday people become conscious, thriving leaders of love.

For further guidance, inspiration, and resources, you can find her at:
VeronicaKrestow.com